THE FOCUS FACTOR

8 Essential
Twenty-First Century Thinking Skills
for Deeper Student Learning

THE FOCUS FACTOR

8 Essential Twenty-First Century Thinking Skills for Deeper Student Learning

James A. Bellanca

TEACHERS COLLEGE PRESS

Teachers College, Columbia University
New York and London

Published by Teachers College Press, 1234 Amsterdam Avenue, New York, NY 10027

Library of Congress Cataloging-in-Publication Data can be obtained at www.loc.gov

ISBN 978-0-8077-5448-1 (paper)

Printed on acid-free paper

Manufactured in the United States of America

20 19 18 17 16 15 14 13 8 7 6 5 4 3 2 1

Contents

INTRODUCTION

The Journey to Deeper Learning

This book is meant to help teachers return American education to the front seat in a world class. Its intent is to help teachers *focus* their daily attention on the implementation of those practical and proven strategies that will most help them attend to a new and necessary priority for every classroom: the thinking, problem solving, and deeper learning skills aligned with the Common Core State Standards that provide the best chance for all students to become deeper learners in the twenty-first century's global economy.

Right now in America, our out-of-sight dropout rate, our middle-of-the-pack international test scores, our dwindling number of college graduates accepted into our own graduate schools, and a radically changed job market have made the case that American education no longer sits in the front row in the global classroom. While a few ostriches may choose to close their ears and eyes to the facts behind these claims, what does stand out is the grave concern expressed by voices, mostly outside of the education community, about the preponderance of our graduates' lack of readiness for advanced education in the twenty-first century's technologically driven global economy. For all the talk about what leaders must do, it will be teachers who drive the changes.

The arrival of the Common Core State Standards was like an alarm clock ringing for K–12 educators. That signal flashed the news that the concerns rattling outside school walls are serious, well-founded, and deserve a substantive response in every classroom. These standards announce that now is the hour for a new theory of action in each and every classroom. It is time, we are told, for teachers to guide daily instruction with two essential elements for teaching and learning that were all but banned by the narrow instructional focus of the outdated

No Child Left Behind era. Those elements are what advocates for 21st-century models of instruction call "critical thinking" and "problem solving." Why? The answer given is "so that our students have the quality of instruction that leads to the deeper learning outcomes for all children in a global economy."

The Common Core Standards make it easy for teachers to focus on their instruction with a balanced approach. This balanced approach will make it possible to push classroom lessons beyond the minimum expectations for surface learning that were a millstone around teachers' necks in the 20th century. The balance promises to allow them to teach for, about, and with higher order thinking in almost every lesson. It also allows for learning outcomes to reflect the deeper learning competencies that an increasing number of our global competitors are adding to their curricula, instruction, and assessment.

Focus is the factor that will most enable teachers to prioritize choices about what and how to achieve balanced instruction. 20th-century curriculum models were a mishmash of skills and information divided into facts that students saw as unconnected and disjointed. That century's fact-driven standardized tests exacerbated this problem.

In contrast, by focusing on deeper learning outcomes, this century's teachers can pay the most attention by balancing instruction of the learning-to-learn skills recommended by the Hewlett Foundation within the teaching of the Common Core State Standards-identified content. The 21st-century skills, especially critical thinking and problem solving, are prerequisites to ever more demanded deeper learning outcomes.

No longer do teachers have to worry that the teaching of critical thinking and problem solving skills detract from the time allotted for curriculum content. Mastery of these skills is now perceived as an essential means to an end. The sharper students' thinking skills are applied to content, the deeper the meaning students can extract. The ends demand the means. (Pellegrino & Hilton, 2012; PISA, 2012)

By concentrating their attention on a balanced treatment of skills with content, today's best teachers can eliminate extraneous material or obsolete skills. In many regards, less will become more. In English Language Arts (ELA), students may study fewer books. However, if they are going to become the deeper and wider readers called for in the PISA (2012) report, they will need the chance to spend more time learning how to gather and interpret information, challenge assumptions, summarize and communicate new insights, and transfer these skills to whatever reading material they are assigned. Ultimately, teachers will focus on these identified skills rather than on recalling the facts of a story on a bubble test.

By concentrating on how to perform key research-targeted reading tasks well, students will be better prepared for the new standardized tests. They will learn how to look less for content knowledge and more for efficient, focused thinking called for by different items. "The key to standardized test reading comprehension is not deep and nuanced insight, but rather an efficient allocation of the student's attention to the elements that really matter" (PISA, 2009).

The same will be said for other curricular content. In Math, the standards narrow the field to place emphasis on key concepts that teachers will have the opportunity to put into practice. As with the ELA standards, the mathematics standards focus the spotlight as much on reasoning and problem solving as they do on mathematics concepts.

THE BALANCED APPROACH IN PRACTICE

The balanced approach to teaching with the Common Core Standards as the framework for instruction is contained in each standard's statement. Each statement is a sentence that starts with a verb such as *analyze, compare, or solve.* More than 80% of these verbs are action words that call for learners to use higher order critical thinking and problem solving about the direct object of the sentence. The English Language Arts Standard, Literature, Grade 5, #3: "Compare and contrast two or more characters, settings, or events in a story or drama, drawing on specific details in the text (e.g., how characters interact)" illustrates this practice.

Since the days of Aristotle, Plato, and Confucius, strong teachers have valued critical thinking and problem solving as essential teaching and learning tools. In the No Child Left Behind decades, advocates of school improvement who favored the mechanistic theories of McGregor and his followers, sought to accentuate teaching practices that prized memory and recall of easily countable factual knowledge. Pushed by calls for increased accountability, they glorified the fast-fading assembly-line production model so that the teacher's job was to read scripts, to push out widgets of information, and to use single-word worksheets that contained countable facts. There was no room on that work sheet assembly line for thinking and problem solving by either those who were working on the line, the teachers, or its so called products, the students.

A new, balanced perspective found in the Common Core State Standards honors critical thinking and problem solving both as tools for learning and as desired end products. There are two reasons for this. First, modern mind and brain research informs educators that these skill sets are the engines of deeper learning (Pellegrino & Hilton, 2012). Like jet propulsion engines, critical thinking and problem solving push the rockets of learning to higher and far more distant targets. Models of knowing that claim memorizing information is the only available engine are as outdated as the first fire arrows launched by the Chin Tartars in 1232 AD. Second, these two complementary skill sets, critical thinking and problem solving, have a life-long learning value. These sets are not only necessary to help today's students master this century's prescribed curriculum content as framed by the new standards, but also to set students up with the capability to progress through deeper life-long learning challenges into higher education and the fast shifting workplace.

The challenge to develop students' complex thinking skills and apply them to mastery of the standards-aligned content as called for in the Common Core framework pushes teachers well beyond what most have been prepared to do. Teachers in schools today are still limited to the practice of those obsolete models of instruction that focus mostly on recall and regurgitation. This is what most of the preservice and professional development of the past 2 decades has emphasized. In elementary schools, direct instruction has been the most glorified and adopted model. Even when gussied up with smart boards, group work, one-to-one computers, click responders, artificial engagement techniques, active learning, and other faddish attention-grabbing tricks, the aim of instruction never changed: students were to memorize math figures and formulas and read for facts to be tested in various subject areas–the better the recall, the higher the grade. This is now described as "surface learning" (Pellegrino & Hilton, 2012).

In middle and secondary grades, the lecture continues to dominate as too many students "sit and git" information from their "expert" sages on the stage. That model has not changed since Abelard and his peers lectured in the Middle Ages.

Today, as children advance out of the primary classroom, it is increasingly probable that they will see piles of worksheets and hear teacher talk at them take up more and more instructional time. When various special effects such as the smart board, videos, digital worksheets, and hands-on activities fail to help students memorize for their short answer, quick recall tests, teachers are formed into professional learning communities to figure out how more of the same type of instruction with slight variations such as one-to-one tutoring might prepare more students to recall testable material that misses deeper understanding.

It is not easy for a teacher to transform shallow instruction to achieve deeper learning outcomes. This is especially true when a teacher works in a school culture that replicates obsolete approaches designed to prepare students for tests in a recall curriculum. Deeper learning instruction works less when school leaders show little interest in encouraging teachers to adopt methods that not only result in significant academic gains, but also provide students with the 21st-century skills to engage in deeper learning or target deeper learning outcomes.

Be that as it may, this book traces a different path for teachers: the path to deeper learning. Deeper learning is lined with theory, with the research that shows its importance, and with examples of research supported best practices. The path is marked by eight essential cognitive skills, the eight competencies or proficiencies that are the foundation of thinking and problem solving in the classroom:

The Eight Essential Cognitive Skills

1. Focus Factor
2. Defining the Problem
3. Making Systematic Searches
4. Asking Questions
5. Making Connections
6. Making Judgments
7. Seeking Alternatives
8. Problem Solving

The first suggested practices provide examples of basic tools for necessary instructional shifts. These practices focus on the mediated learning skills that say "you can't ignore student thinking if you want deeper learning." The practices provide basic tools for teachers to attend to how they develop standards-aligned thinking skills in the curriculum. After these easy-to-adopt strategies, more complex strategies take teachers into the development of practical tools that facilitate students' problem solving competencies. It is these that are most crucial, the research is showing, for moving students to the much desired deeper learning of the 21st-century curriculum.

In a comprehensive study of deeper learning released in July 2012, *Education for Life and Work: Developing Transferable Knowledge and Skills in the 21st Century*, the National Research Council described deeper learning as that which results when students are able to apply critical thinking and problem solving skills to rigorous content and transfer these skills to other areas in the curriculum and out-of-school situations. Deeper learning instruction intends that all students master standards-aligned academic content, think critically and solve complex problems, work collaboratively, communicate effectively, learn how to learn, and self-direct the transfer of these skills from the classroom forward to whatever advanced education they select and to the real work world (Pellegrino & Hilton, 2012).

This book is a practical resource guide for helping teachers return critical thinking and problem solving to Common Core classrooms by allowing them to become facilitators of deeper learning. The text highlights the mediation of students' cognitive functions and operations.

As readers progress through these chapters, some will discover, "I already do that." My first response to this statement would be a sincere and hearty "Wonderful!" I will follow the exclamation with, "And as you will discover, you will have the opportunity to review and refine what you already do well so that you can enrich students' learning faster and better with intentional attention to these 21st-century skills as the main goal of your Common Core instruction. I will also ask you to advocate for what you are doing by informing those who doubt the effectiveness of your approach. Show them the research and broadcast its importance for your students."

My second response would build on the first. I would encourage these readers to polish and expand their repertoire of teaching skills for helping students develop critical thinking and problem solving not as something that occurs now and then, but that is a daily occurrence. Their goal would be to bring every student to the point that he or she is deeply engaged each and every day in deeper learning as the *primary* instructional thrust of the classroom. To this end, I would hope that all would transfer the ideas of this book and initiate a restructuring of instruction that reflects the most personally relevant ideas. This transfer could begin by considering that the major rationale for adding more of these skills into daily lessons is to help students escape the bonds of the recall curriculum and to find ways to give equal time to the intentional development of critical thinking and problem solving so you and all of your students can produce deeper learning outcomes.

If by chance any of the content of this book is totally new to any who read it, I would urge them to return to the first chapter or to one other chapter that strikes them as what their students need the most. After they have read the entire book, I would encourage those readers to plan how they could focus on the chapter's target skill over the next few months, to work backward, planning the action steps that they will introduce to get all students to deeper learning outcomes.

NEW TOOLS FOR A NEW CENTURY

In my first years of teaching, my mentors helped me adopt four basic teaching principles:

1. All students benefit by developing their thinking and problem solving skills, including those students who I was told by their records "couldn't."
2. There is a substantive difference between challenging students to think by providing a rigorous reading and writing curriculum that *assumes* critical thinking might "rub off" just because the material is tougher versus *being intentional* about the teaching of specific thinking skills (such as analysis or comparison) that ensured every student would develop those skills to tackle that tougher material and become skillful problem solvers and deeper learners. Both approaches are important, I learned, but the second is essential to reach the goal of deeper learning.
3. Sharpened thinking and problem solving are important for every student, but not as important as the ability to *transfer* that thinking to better master the curriculum being studied in my classroom and others through the school day. Successful transfer of concepts and skills is the heart and soul of deeper learning.

4. The value of each approach in producing deeper learning—the goal stands alone. There are a variety of paths to that goal, not a single yellow brick road.

This book illustrates that teachers can rely on proven mind-expanding practices that enable students to integrate critical and creative thinking skills for the purpose of solving crucial, academic, and real-world problems much in the manner that such innovative thinkers as Thomas Edison, Jane Goodall and Steve Jobs did. It proposes to help teachers master practical ways to improve how students connect the dots, that is, how students effectively manage the disparate, fast-flowing information which they are required to sort and synthesize every fact-saturated day, develop thinking skills, strengthen cognitive functions, and join all together like many streams into a single river flowing to the ocean. In every case, the strategies called for will assist teachers in aligning what they teach within the Common Core framework.

As teachers take advantage of what is offered in the following chapters, they can focus on these key points:

- *The resolve* to persist in helping students connect the 21st-century learning dots by explicitly and intentionally linking students' abilities to think and problem solve within rigorous content framed by the Common Core Standards. This resolve requires the three Ps: planning, persistence, and purposeful practice of these skills over time—so that students can internalize their new skills.
- *The mediation* of those thinking processes that enable students to connect the dots. Mediation occurs when there is a clear intention to help students make the connections that result in their understanding of deeper meanings in the curriculum that they are able to transfer. The Chinese proverb that distinguishes between fishing and teaching how to fish applies here. The 21st-century teacher as mediator is all about teaching students how to fish, not doing the fishing for them.
- *The process* of helping students uncover meaning, how they make sense of the dots they see through use of skillful questioning and mindful feedback that leads to transfer. Feedback is especially important when it spotlights how well students are seeing the explicit connection between individual thinking skills and the macro-process of problem solving.

- *The strategies* identified to mediate the students' dot connecting in their curriculum are important, but less so than the first three points just made. A variety of tactics allows teachers to guide practice over time within plans to develop students' self-directed learning dispositions.
- *The technology*—the teaching tools which are uniquely available in the 21st century to help teachers develop students' problem-solving skills within the curriculum. Like other best teaching practices, technology's many manifestations enrich teaching and learning, but neither hardware, software, nor the Internet are skills in themselves. Learning to use these tools requires unique skills, some of which must be explicitly developed, especially if the tools are going to enrich thinking, problem solving, and mastery of the curriculum.
- *The content* is the dot that enables the students to ground and then transfer the new meanings they have uncovered. As a result of following a problem solving scenario to investigate standards-aligned content as the driving force of the 21st-century learning paradigm, students can end with a deeper understanding of the material examined, greater mastery of the ever emerging technology tools, and the dispositions to challenge the most difficult problems in and outside the classroom with their strengthened thinking and problem-solving skills.

Mediating Matters of the Mind

The three Ms (mediate, matter, mind) send the message of what is most important if American schools are to return to their top-performing leadership in the 21st century's global economy. This book is a practical guide designed to start toward that end those who are most crucial for making all minds matter: classroom teachers. The second is to focus first on the cognitive functions that are the essential prerequisite proficiencies or competencies students need as the skeleton supporting their complex thinking skills. The book is one piece of a larger puzzle. The study and application of this book's practical ideas, along with its explanations of theory, research, and other rationales to solve the problem of how to transform day-to-day instruction, intends to help teachers who accept the book's assumptions to replace obsolete methods. It is meant to give them tools to replace recall and regurgitation with strategies that intentionally develop critical thinking and problem solving.

CHAPTER STRUCTURE AND CONTENT

The Big Picture: The Focus Factor

In Chapter 5, the focus factor is the focus. It delves into the background, the benefits, and then the strategies that encourage individuals to concentrate, make priorities, and look to go into a few skills and key concepts more deeply, rather than cover the curriculum. Because focus is such an essential thinking skill, one that is closely connected to the development of self-directed learners who are able to control the quality of their thinking and be responsible for the development of their own deeper thinking abilities, this chapter sits in the center of the chapters. It also provides a thread that weaves its way through every chapter.

Readers of this book will do no harm if they make focus the key factor that influences their instruction on critical thinking, and problem solving for deeper learning.

The Chapters

The first two chapters of this book discuss the what and why, the background of intentional, explicit development of thinking and problem-solving skills in the 21st century's standards-aligned classroom. The remaining chapters focus on specific skills with an emphasis on how teachers can help their students to reach the goal of deeper learning.

Each chapter focuses on a thinking or problem-solving skill. After an exposition on the chapter's target skill, the second part of the chapter guides the reader through easy to adopt starter strategies. These starters are the practical, tested, interactive, and hands-on strategies that teachers can adapt to introduce the targeted thinking and problem-solving skills. Recommended application ages are labeled "elementary." "middle," and "secondary" but are not meant to be definitive. Next, more extensive strategies and lesson or project designs are suggested so that teachers may plan how to give the balanced time and attention to the targeted skill that will assist students with internalizing the skill and taking increased responsibility for its transfer across the curriculum and into out-of-school situations. Finally, a summary and a guided reflection close out each chapter.

Chapter 1: New Challenges for a New Century. As happened in the years after the printing press was invented, the 21st century presents new challenges for the new age's teaching and learning paradigm. This chapter introduces how those challenges are captured in a need for deeper learning for all students and new tools for teaching for teachers.

Chapter 2: Mediating Matters of the Mind illustrates the reasons for balancing the 21st-century curriculum with intentional and explicit development of critical thinking and problem-solving skills for all students.

Chapter 3: Solving Loose Problems for Deeper Learning begins by distinguishing the various types of problem solving in the Common Core Standards before introducing ways to help students learn how to define problems and select strategies for solving them.

Chapter 4: Defining Problems: An Essential Prerequisite focuses on the mediation for helping students learn what some consider as the quintessential sub-skill in problem solving: the definition of the problem. It attends to the development of other cognitive functions problem solvers can rely on as they work to turn loose problems into tightly structured problems with a strong problem statement. These functions are used as criteria for assessing the quality of a problem definition.

Chapter 5: The Focus Factor identifies the benefits of helping students sharpen their abilities to focus their thinking in order to discriminate among the multiple information sources that bombard them. It continues with related strategies that decrease impulsivity and increase reflection.

Chapter 6: Toward More Systematic Searches defines the meaning and value of systematic thinking, especially when students are seeking online information. Practical steps to help students make systematic searches follow.

Chapter 7: Asking Productive Questions. In the information age, students need to develop their questioning skills. Using the Common Core Standards as a guide, teachers can introduce students to essential, guiding, probing, and assessing questions.

Chapter 8: Making Connections, Making Sense. Inference making is one of the most practical and important critical thinking skills a student can develop. The skill's use jumpstarts reading comprehension and expands across the curriculum. Practical strategies in this chapter provide teachers with tools to focus on explicit development of the skills for making sense.

Chapter 9: Making Judgment Calls provides strategies to develop students' abilities to judge information found on- and off-line. Transfer tactics provide practical tools to help students build good judgment skills in other areas as well.

Chapter 10: There's Always a Better Way introduces the key creative thinking skills that are necessary for innovative problem solving. Tactics help teachers promote new ways of thinking to go with the critical thinking skills that make for effective problem solving.

Chapter 11: Mediating Problem Solving for Deeper Learning provides practical suggestions for transferring critical and creative thinking skills into the defining and solving of loosely structured problems in order to achieve deeper learning. Special emphasis is placed on creating students' dispositions or mindsets to be problem solvers and deep learners.

A final focus point. At the end of each chapter, you will find a section called "Connecting the Dots," a framework for gathering the most important ideas from the text, organizing the concepts so they make the most sense, and planning action steps. The final chapter of the book also allows you to focus on the most relevant ideas from all the chapters and organize them for a personal transfer plan.

CHAPTER 1

New Challenges for a New Century

If we teach today's students as we taught yesterday's, we rob them of tomorrow.

—John Dewey

In this second decade of the 21st century, important voices have made many, many pronouncements about the need for American schools to adapt curriculum and instruction practices to ones more able to prepare today's graduates for tomorrow's global economy. One important source even labeled our schools' curriculum and instruction as "obsolete" (Stewart, 2006). Most advocate for an American curriculum saturated with what the Partnership for 21st Century Skills (P21) is calling the four Cs and the three Rs: critical thinking, creative problem solving, collaboration, and communication with a curriculum that is rigorous, relevant, and results directed (P21, 2012). P21's call implies that the four Cs and three Rs are not new to the teaching and learning stage. What is new is the tenor of the times.

For many reasons, this new century is not the one our grandparents, or even our parents, knew. It is a new era, filled with new challenges, the intensity of which students have not experienced since Gutenberg's press shook the learning world in 1450.

VOICES OF CONCERN

U.S. student results from the 2003 Program for International Student Achievement's (PISA) results in mathematical problem solving, literacy, science, financial literacy, and cross-curricular problem-solving exams provoked much consternation in American business, government, and education circles. Following a 1992 PISA report that raised the bar for learning standards for 15-year-olds from 30 nations, more than two dozen reports from U.S. organizations called for schools to place the four Cs and three Rs as the headline on the first page in the curriculum. Among others, the American Management Association, McGraw Hill Research Foundation, and the American College Testing Service analyzed PISA and other data prior to publishing their reactions. They agreed that the now-named 21st-century skills were essential for students to live, learn, and thrive in the technology-saturated 21st-century work world and to produce an American workforce able to compete in the new and rapidly changing global economy.

Responding to these voices, the National Governor's Association and the Council of Chief State School Officers spearheaded the development of a new set of national learning standards. These Common Core State Standards were meant to replace the many sets of standards in each state, to raise U.S. standards to the heights achieved by countries such as Finland, Singapore, Canada, Australia, and other nations whose PISA test results exceeded U.S. performances. To back these Common Core Standards with more rigorous assessments, the U.S. Department of Education funded two multistate testing consortia. With new national tests from the Partnership for Assessment of Readiness for College and Careers (PARCC) and the Smarter Balanced Assessment Consortium (SBAC), the aim was to push schools to make significant adjustments in curriculum, instruction, and assessment and to provide instruction for all students that aligned with the international standards. The desired outcome was a more universal development of American students' 21st-century skills within a more rigorous curriculum.

Highlighting schools' traditional heavy emphasis on testing for recall, the late 20th century's educational paradigm, the voices argued that our schools have failed the most recent student generations (American College Testing Service, 2012). These critics alleged that the emphasis on teaching students to recall and regurgitate facts failed to close the achievement gap or lower this nation's world-leading dropout rate. Worse yet, it increased the amount of wasted test-prep time for even the most advanced placement students. (Wagner, 2010)

Faculty at American higher education institutions added their voices. They had long complained that too many incoming freshmen were intellectually unprepared for the rigors of complex post-secondary classrooms. Although a few high-performing high schools are known to have over-prepared their graduates, most students entering college from American high schools were said to lack even the most rudimentary learning skills. As evidence, higher education voices noted how plague-like numbers of freshmen required remedial tutoring help (Meier, 2011). Add to these statistics the expanding numbers of American high school graduates who drop out in their first year of college and the increasing number of students from other countries who are taking seats in undergraduate and graduate schools, and it is easy to see the challenge American teachers face with what PBS's *Frontline* called the "Dropout Nation" (Schneider & Lin, 2011; *Frontline*, 2012).

A NEW WORLD OUTSIDE SCHOOL WALLS

Fast forward from today's school desks to the world beyond classroom borders. There, additional evidence adds fuel to the notion that the global village is undergoing significant changes. Inside the school walls, complexions and accented English announce that the classroom is reflecting the continuing shift in American society to a student population that is more diverse than it has ever been. In the world outside school walls, today's students are flooded with information like no prior generation. Data surround them. Spreadsheets, e-mails, blogs, tweets, and texts are everywhere at every moment. Smart phones and "dumb" phones are glued to young folks' ears. TV and online ads assault their young consumer heads. . . and pockets. In this time of information overload, there is no time for young people to learn what will really prepare them for a future that only promises greater information tsunamis.

In 2012, a new hot-burning log was thrown on the fire. The Organization for Economic Cooperation and Development's (OECD) 34-member-nation representatives who oversee PISA elected to increase the heat. For the first time, PISA 2012 added a framework for cross-curricular problem solving that assessed not only the mathematic reasoning skills tested in 2003, but also how well students were able to apply creative and critical thinking skills to real world problem scenarios that are outside the school curricula.

For the first time, American students and those from the other participating nations faced nonmathematical, ill-defined problems and used technology to show their intellectual competencies at four levels of performance. Just as the early PISA exams raised the bar in schools around the globe and caused the United States to rethink its schooling in the light of more rigorous global standards agreed to be more stringent than its own, it is highly predictable that this most recent PISA rendition will have a similar negative effect. This time the effect spotlights critical and creative thinking as these skill sets impact students' practical problem-solving competencies across knowledge domains such as science, language arts, social studies, and even the arts. Even if it takes several years for the PISA effect to trickle down to U.S. test makers, it is also predictable that within the coming decade, all U.S. students will face an equally rigorous testing regimen.

A PATH OF HOPE: NEW INSIGHTS FROM NEW NEURO RESEARCH

The burgeoning research fields that are unleashing new knowledge about the human brain present additional challenges to the fields of teaching and learning. Neuroscientific research completed outside the education community has grown rapidly in early years of this century, especially in brain studies of the young, the elderly, and those with cognitive challenges (Feuerstein, Feuerstein, & Falik, 2010). From this increasing number of studies, educators have begun to discover information pools that *suggest* new benefits that should be available for all learners. Although at this point, brain research in education lags in providing strong *empirical* data with wide applicability, there are key elements of brain research that strongly suggest that all students are capable of more, faster, and deeper learning than ever imagined 50 years ago.

It is intentional, explicit instruction of the complex cognitive strategies, including the macro-process of inquiry and investigation identified for high effects on achievement (Marzano Research Lab, 2012) that first drew attention to the value of more inquiry, investigation, and invention to solve problems. These are connected with other teaching tools for explicit skill instruction in hypothesis testing, proving, asking questions, and comparing. Although in the pre-tech age, there were teachers who adopted explicit instruction for teaching thinking skills by following their gut instincts, the vault of research that exists today provides reassuring support that these pioneers were on the right track. In addition, other bodies of related research have signaled the importance of teaching about thinking whether students are completing offline or online assignments.

Especially important are studies from the emerging field of mind, brain, and education sciences, and continuing research on the best teaching practices. First, most recently there is the research about "deeper learning." The National Research Council's report on this concept defines deeper learning as "the process through which a person becomes capable of taking what was learned in one situation and applying it to new situations." The report goes further to describe how this deeper learning process is what enables students to develop 21st-century competencies that they are able to transfer within a given subject area, including both knowledge and skills (Pellegrino & Hilton, 2012).

Central to this study are the data showing that learning is more than the collection of facts for the memory. Yes, knowledge recall is one important component of learning. The memory is one important element in the brain. But there are at least five other components that contribute to what the authors call "deeper learning." They suggest that just because a child knows math facts (an important task) and can circle a correct fact on a worksheet, there is no assurance that the child can use this factual knowledge to solve even the most rudimentary one-step word problem. Being able *to solve* a one-step word problem, one of the simplest acts of close transfer, will not usually happen without a teacher's or parent's intentional direction in how to move this known fact into practice. The same holds true, of course, for more complex transfer problems that students will face every day as they proceed through more challenging curriculum and into other outside situations.

The deeper learning that this report suggests must be the principal goal of teaching and learning in 21st-century classrooms, and what the PISA Problem Solving Exams assess, is more complex than recall-based learning inherited from past centuries. There is also the implication that teachers will need to make major adjustments in their instruction so that they can prepare every child to:

1. Master core academic content
2. Think critically and solves complex problems
3. Work collaboratively
4. Communicate effectively

5. Learn how to learn (e.g., self-directed learning) and, most important,
6. Transfer these skills from one real world situation to another (Hewlett Foundation, 2012; Pellegrino & Hilton, 2012).

In a like manner, the transfer of the knowledge base of brain research to classroom practice holds great promise for teachers who are ready to adjust how they teach to this century's new challenges. Among the growing information stores most ready for that transfer, teachers can find proven brain-enriching practices from a variety of sources including the following:

Prior knowledge. Neuroscientist and grade 6–12 educator Judy Willis makes clear how activities selected by teachers can assist in building patterns from prior knowledge that make sense. When active engagement of the mind from such tactics as graphic organizers, analogies, and brainstorming, and multisensory tasks are employed, the stored memory and the hippocampus connect to expand the knowledge base (Willis, 2010).

Reading comprehension. Brain imaging has shown the complexity of this cognitive task. Unfortunately, inclusion of intentional cognitive instruction to develop comprehension at the early ages is given a back seat in many U.S. classrooms. Thus, students may acquire the mechanics or procedures for reading well, but not the linkages needed to understand the material that they read nor improve the requisite skills (Coch & Ansari, 2006).

Role of emotion in solving loose problems. Students given a significant choice such as occurs when they were confronted with "loose" or "messy" problems in problem-based learning scenarios, bring strong emotions to bear on the cognitive challenges these problems present. Studies suggest that the depth and complexity of open-ended tasks are important factors in brain development, especially when teachers foster making connections to the material and manage the socioemotional climate of the classroom (Immordino-Yang, Chiao, & Fiske, 2010).

Role of the teacher as learning mediator. Central to the teacher's role as mediator in the learning process is the modeling of skillful thinking. When teachers probe students' thinking ("Tell me why you think that . . ." or, "Please give me an example of what you mean . . ."), their probing to deepen students' thinking via such reflective questioning cues students to apply their thinking at increased levels of difficulty. For instance, instead of asking students to summarize facts, they can challenge the students to compare the facts or evaluate the summary. Indeed, mirroring studies of the brain's neurons confirm the importance of the resulting patterned repetitions in these mediated learning experiences (Rizzolati & Arbib, 1998; Buccino et al., 2004).

Technology as a driver of teaching and learning. Although technology is not the be-all and the end-all for advancing student learning, there is no doubt that harnessed appropriately, technology is as large and powerful a leap forward as was the printing press (Schacter, 1999; Lemke, 2011). Technology does provide tools, each of which has its own set of skill demands. Some of the tools facilitate critical and creative thinking and contribute to problem solving. The impact of these tools on problem solving can be heightened by skillful teachers. When teachers mediate the thinking and problem solving that students do through technology tools, they are likely to speed and deepen students' mastery of the tools. Take as an example, the wiki. This tool enables students to collaborate on researching and writing about a common topic. Using a jigsaw model, different groups of students concentrate on different studies about a topic such as sustainability in the ecosystem. One team digs deep on the history; another on the science, and so forth. With the wiki, they can contribute to each other's gathered information, make comments, edit, and so forth. Their facility with the digital tool increases, as does their ability to evaluate information, make sense of ideas, and problem solve, all simultaneously.

In addition to these specific connections, best practices such as inquiry (Darling-Hammond, 2011), project and problem-based learning (Ravitz, 2009), technology (Lemke,2011), gaming (Holt, 1999), and content-free thinking skills (Ben Hur, 2006) align with brain/mind studies. Each study provides informative insights about what happens when sufficient time is devoted to teaching students how to think, collaborate, and communicate, not for each skill's isolated sake, but for solving problems about the authentic, real world and accomplishing deeper learning outcomes. In addition, the list of high-effect teaching strategies that are most likely to increase student achievement include instruction that promotes hypothesizing, comparing, inquiring, and investigating aligned with the Common Core Standards, the four Cs, and with brain studies (Bellanca, Fogarty, & Pete, 2012).

IN SUMMARY

Many outside the school walls have voiced legitimate concerns about American schools' perceived loss of value. Various pieces of evidence, not the least of which has been the assertions by American corporations that they are unable to hire "cheaper" employees and are unable to hire sufficient numbers of our graduates into the jobs that will keep this nation economically competitive in the expanding global economy, have stirred the pot. Add to these corporate voices the challenge of the 2012 PISA exams, that which will assess cross-curricular problem-solving competencies for the first time and additional concerns emerge. On the other hand, the Common Core State Standards, PARCC and Smarter Balance Tests, and a growing body of research on what practices will enable teachers to address development of the skill sets our students need to perform competitively show great promise for addressing the concerns about the capabilities of our students to succeed in higher education and the 21st-century global workplace.

Connecting the Dots

- List the three ideas from this chapter that are most meaningful to you.
- Explain why you selected each of these ideas.
- How might you transfer these ideas to your work with 21st-century learners?

In times of change, it is the learners that will inherit the earth while the learned will find themselves beautifully equipped for a world that no longer exists.

—Eric Hoffer

CHAPTER 2

Mediating Matters of the Mind

What children can do with the assistance of others might be in some sense even more indicative of their mental development than what they can do alone.

—Lev Vygotsky

Imagine two mothers preparing to bake bread:

- One says to her children, "Jon, you go to the counter. There's everything you'll need to bake bread. Maria, you go to that other counter. Your supplies are there. I will work here. Let me know when you are done."
- The other takes a different tack: "I want you both to join me here, one on each side. I want you to listen to my questions so that you can learn by my example. My first question to you both . . .When you see all these materials, what do you think we are going to do?"

From the start, there is an important, subtle difference in each mother's teaching approach. The first takes a laissez-faire approach that puts the children on their own, letting them do their own thing. The second mediates the children's learning as an experience that begins with an open-ended question. As the children respond, she poses additional open-ended questions that guide or mediate their learning experience.

Mediated learning experience is a term that cognitive psychologist Reuven Feuerstein introduced to describe what a teacher or parent does when explicitly enabling children to improve their natural tendencies to think well and apply sharpened thinking skills to solve relevant everyday problems. The adults do so without telling children answers or leaving the children to learn how to swim on their own. (Feuerstein, Feuerstein, & Falik, 2010).

Feuerstein emphasized that a caring, questioning adult is like the driver of a learning bus that traverses the city making sure that the passengers get to their destinations most expeditiously. Parents and teachers prompt learners' thinking with questions and clues; children do the thinking and problem solving to find *their* own solutions.

The teacher or parent as mediator stands between the student and the material (e.g., a two-step number operation problem, the principle of buoyancy, the character of Huck Finn) and helps the student extract the thinking skills needed to understand that material or the problem (e.g., *prove* the solution, *give reasons* for the principle, *analyze* the character). So that students can learn to apply as well as name the targeted thinking skill, the mediator asks productive questions to *spotlight* the thinking verb ("Can I *compare* thee to a summer's day?") separating it from the direct object ("a summer's day"). With additional clues, the teacher uses open-ended questions from the upper floors of Bloom's taxonomy, focuses the student's mind on that verb, unpacking what it means and what mental steps are taken to complete the mental menu. Then when it becomes clear that the student understands the "how to" of a particular thinking process, the teacher encourages the student to follow the menu, giving constructive suggestions or asking questions that help the student make sense of the cognitive actions taken and apply that new understanding to solve a problem (e.g., "How is a triangle like a square?" "How is it different?"). Mediators must become adept with "wait time" by not answering their own questions or by announcing answers or solutions to problems prematurely.

Feuerstein's favorite illustration of the learning experience that is "mediated' is like the bread baking story that began this chapter. In this story, each mother takes a toddler to the park. One arrives, unpacks the stroller and sets the child free to play on his own with no purposeful directions. The other does the same, but when she hears a sparrow sing, she pulls the child aside, points to the tree and asks, "What do you see? What do you hear?" More questions follow until the child is able to label the bird with an accurate name.

Feuerstein notes that the child in the second case is the more fortunate. The parent has acted as a collaborative intermediary in mediating the child's thinking process, helping the child to discover faster what he may or may not have noticed on his own, and thus validating Vygotsky's developmental theory that says, "What children can do with the assistance of others might be in some sense even more indicative of their mental development than what they can do alone" (Vygotsky, 1978).

This second, proactive mother, included in her mediation the three identifying behaviors that Feuerstein adopted to distinguish mediation of a learning experience from other teaching acts.

First, the mediator was intentional and asked for a specific response from the child.
Second, the mediator focused on helping the child find meaning in the event.
Third, she helped the child transfer his new understanding into action by labeling the bird sighted.

Feuerstein notes that this mediation process is necessary to sharpen the child's thinking, to extract the thinking out of the tree (the meaningful content) that may be hiding the object from view and helping the learner describe and label what he sees and hears prior to labeling it. With additional mediation, the child reflects on the thinking, thus learning *from* doing. This is different from the role of the mother or teacher who brings the child to the park, but lets the child *discover* whatever he may find or not. It is also different from the mother who points out the bird and might tell the child, "See, that is a sparrow. You know this because I told you so." (Feuerstein et al., 1980).

From this story, Feuerstein is able to define the term he advanced, the mediated learning experience. He describes the specific role of the teacher as a go-between, a purpose-driven guide, a facilitator of a thinking experience that intentionally leads to more effective learning through reflection. In his view, learning and problem solving are synonymous.

Mediation does not steal away other more traditional roles from teachers such as "instructor" or "facilitator." Teachers keep these hats. Feuerstein is merely more insistent and precise about a role that he believes is crucial to the deeper learning demanded of students in the 21st century. It a role that is central to helping students connect the dots: the teacher's mediation of thinking and problem solving to deepen students' understanding of what they are learning. For this to happen, he teaches the importance of the mediator bringing three elements—intentionality with reciprocity, the search for meaning, and the power of transferability—to each and every experience (Feuerstein, Feuerstein, & Falik, 2010).

Mediating Students' Problem Solving Competency

- Intentional with reciprocity
- Meaningful
- Transferable

TWO DEGREES OF MEDIATION—TWO LEVELS OF THINKING

Historically in their treatment of critical thinking and problem solving, schools have emphasized only one category of thinking that connects to effective problem solving: the cognitive operations such as comparing and analyzing. Bloom attended to the operations by creating a hierarchy of six levels so that educators could better classify the cognitive operations in the curriculum. From the time that researchers highlighted the taxonomy as a best practice for increasing achievement such as in the groundbreaking Los Angeles High Expectation Project (Kermin, 1979), this taxonomy has dominated how teachers think about thinking in the curriculum.

The school-important thinking operations such as analyzing, comparing, proving, and predicting function much like the energy source in a centralized heating system. Thanks to recent neurological studies of the brain, what both Vygotsky and Feuerstein have called "cognitive functions" (see Figure 2.1), another set of thinking tools is becoming recognized for its impact on the intentional development of students as problem solvers.

When unattended, undeveloped, or unmediated, Feuerstein concluded that were 26 deficient cognitive functions which were a detriment to learning (Feuerstein et al., 1980; Feuerstein, Feuerstein, & Falik, 2010). He noted that these deficiencies were not cast in concrete. A teacher who has accepted the belief that minds are mutable could learn to adopt mediating practices that will transform deficiencies into powerful, metacognitively rich problem-solving behaviors.

TABLE 2.1. Hierarchy Chart: Applying Feuerstein's Cognitive Functions

The First String	The Second String
Focused Perception	Hypothesizing
Control Impulsive Reactions	Internalizing
Systematic Searches	Labeling
Problem Discovery and Definition	Testing Strategies
Connecting Facts and Concepts	Spatial Orientation
Search for Alternatives	Choosing Frame of Reference
Form and Describe Categories	Temporal Orientation
	Planning
	Conservation of Constancies
	Summarizing a Concept
	Precise Measurement
	Logical Evidence
	Widen Conceptual Field
	Express a Concept
	Integration of Information Sources
	Express a Virtual Relationship
	Relevant Information Selection
	Avoid Trial and Error Guesses
	Spontaneous Comparisons

Source: Feuerstein et al., 1980

Teachers can learn to recognize cognitive functions as *deficient* when they see and hear them blocking students' daily learning attempts.

There are seven deficiencies that stand out most consistently in the school day. These present themselves as weak habits of mind and negatively influence student learning success:

- *Rampant Impulsivity:* The student acts without thought or planning.
- *Disorganization:* The student's locker, desk, and room look as if they were struck by a hurricane.

- *Imprecise and Inaccurate Thought:* The student ignores details and fails to double check facts.
- *Data Distortion:* The student cannot get a fact straight.
- *Episodic Thinking:* The student jumps from idea to idea without ever connecting two thoughts, setting a goal, or making a plan.
- *Illogic:* The student presents unconnected reasons and/or rationalizations to defend a position.
- *Closed Minded:* The student stays locked on one narrow point of view and refuses to consider options.

For Feuerstein, good news celebrates the truism that teachers and parents *can* change students' minds, literally and figuratively. With careful attention, sound modeling, facilitated refinement, and mediated questions that lead students to learn *from* their own thinking, teachers or parents can integrate explicit strategies into daily lessons, change physical structures in the brain and facilitate new mindsets. In the end, deficient functions do become more efficient.

How is this change recognizable? Again, the observation of students' cognitive functions in the positive give the first evidence as intentional interventions to mediate create:

- *Self-Directed Reflectors:* Students who stop to think, set goals, align tasks, and solve increasingly complex problems.
- *Connection Makers:* Students who connect the dots among like facts and ideas.
- *Precise and Accurate Thinkers:* Students who look for exact answers, always double checking facts and figures intending to avoid the tiniest flaw.
- *Systematic Problem Solvers:* Students who rely on logic and proceed through problems with an organized, logical approach that uses multiple creative and critical thinking skills.
- *Minds Open to Ideas:* Students who consider other points of view and are flexible in their problem solving tasks.

Feuerstein's 50 years of practice show that the functions interact with each other. The more often teachers continue their explicit and purposeful development of a student's targeted functions, such as impulse control or precision, the more ready students will advance thinking with the other positive functions such as labeling, conservation of constancy, use of logical evidence, summarizing, and planning.

Teachers prepared to see how and where these cognitive functions serve as prerequisites and partners in the problem-solving process can call upon their mediation skills and blend various cognitive functions during teachable moments that deepen student thinking. With a plan for change that calls for repeated mediation of learning experiences, crystalized cognitive changes become observable on a daily basis.

The repetition of mediated practice over time has special importance. As Pellegrino and Hilton point out in their study of deeper learning (2012), development of cognitive skills requires extended time and repeated practice, in some cases up to 10,000 practice instances, before a cognitive skill becomes a refined habit of mind as hardened as a stalactite.

When it comes time to address the 26 cognitive functions in the classroom, it helps to divide them into two groups. The most important functions each headline a chapter in this book. The secondary functions are intertwined as strategies for advancing the development of the headliners. Functions such as planning, labeling, or finding evidence are no less important than the selected eight. However, they fall into a backup role because they are called upon less frequently in the classroom. Thus, functions such as problem definition, systematic searching, and making connections are presented as first-string starters and receive the bulk of attention and feedback when teachers are addressing the development of a whole class. Individuals whose major dysfunction is found in the backup group can receive individual education plans to focus on that function.

THE THINKING–PROBLEM SOLVING CONNECTION

Problem solving is like a giant bakery counter. Its sweets are divided into many sections separated from the breads. Shoppers can pick and choose depending on their needs of the moment. For effective problem solving in the curriculum, the range of thinking skills is also wide and deep. An astute teacher is not deterred by the number of choices. By learning how to identify, classify, and evaluate the thinking skills appropriate for her students' problem-solving proficiency, she is able to integrate the right thinking skills into the right spots in her curriculum, align these skills with the standards, and thus develop her students' problem-solving proficiency.

The problem-solving proficiency is a set of thinking skills, identified most simply as those that enable students to achieve a desired goal that results in a novel solution. This skill set includes the convergent operations of analyzing, comparing and contrasting, defining, classifying, distinguishing, differentiating, and making judgments. It also includes such divergent thinking operations as idea generating, hypothesizing, predicting, producing, and estimating. As brain images have shown, these convergent and divergent skills interact, switch positions, and inform each other throughout the problem-solving process even as individual minds spawn different solutions with different content. In this regard, the thinking skills are the prerequisite and interconnected processes inherent in productive problem solving (PISA, 2012).

How the thinking skills connect in a problem-solving scenario is not a random accident. It is a purposeful, intentional connecting of the dots. "Connect the dots" is a metaphor about making sense of information that appears random or unorganized. The metaphor helps with the understanding of how the mind integrates thinking skills within the problem-solving framework that students are likely to face on an increased basis as this century advances. More and more, the phrase "connect the dots" is quoted in daily news stories, magazine articles, titles, and ads. Pundits and politicians repeat it. The metaphor suggests how making sense of the millions of bits and pieces of information that fly about every day is more important than during any preceding century.

At home and at work, the number one challenge for citizens is finding the best ways to connect disparate dots so they can understand past events, predict future occurrences, identify thinking gaps and biases, and propose innovative solutions to real world problems. Problems may be simple such as solving the puzzle for operating a new carafe-less coffee maker, taking video with the latest model smart phone, or determining how to start a keyless automobile without a printed instruction book. Or, they may include complex issues that deal with decreasing phone-use-related car accidents, eradicating invasive fish from local rivers, or eliminating bullies from a schoolyard.

Many are the events in history where the dots weren't connected. What was Napoleon thinking at Waterloo? Who at Ford thought the Edsel was the *next* generation? And what can we say of the thinking inside Lehman Brothers, Enron, and Pan Am Airways? Whatever happened to Betamax?

History has also shown how skill in connecting dots, making sense of diverse, almost invisible bits and pieces of information, asking the right questions, and making sound judgments opened new windows of opportunity. Bill Gates did it. So did Warren Buffet, Steve Jobs, Mother Teresa, Mark Zuckerberg, Mahatma Gandhi, and Maya Angelou. Some like J.K. Rowling, Oprah Winfrey, and Martin Luther King, Jr. connected multiple dots of failure before they discovered their dots of success.

Every field of human endeavor has faced great problem-solving challenges that required critical and creative thinking responses to solve big problems. Scientists look into their microscopes or experiment with their lasers to discover answers to important questions. Salk, Goodall, Curie, Pasteur, Copernicus, and Hagen are but a few who followed dots that often lead to dead ends before they experienced success. With persistent questioning, systematic searching, focus, reflection, and logic, each one's inquiry lead to an amazing result that spotlighted smart thinking and skillful problem solving.

IN SUMMARY

Enlightened by the research on brain development, high-effects teaching strategies and deeper learning, this era's teachers have a ripe opportunity to add skills to their repertoires. As they are called upon to balance standards-aligned instruction with more explicit and intentional attention to students' thinking and problem-solving skills, they are ready to be mediators of deeper learning experiences.

Cognitive psychologist Reuven Feuerstein labels this role "mediator of learning experiences" because of the value he places on teachers guiding and directing what and how students learn (Feuerstein, Feuerstein, & Falik, 2010). When wearing this hat, teachers focus students' concentrated attention on the cognitive functions that are the prerequisites of learning and the cognitive operations that are the driving engine for problem solving. Although few teachers have been prepared formally to assume this role, the tools do exist for them to learn how to do so.

Connecting the Dots

- List the three ideas from this chapter that hold the most meaning for you.
- Explain why you selected of these ideas.How might you transfer these ideas to your work with 21st-century learners?

Everything is mediated through the mind, translated, filtered, allegorized, twisted, even falsified by it.

—C.J. Jung

CHAPTER 3

Solving Loose Problems for Deeper Learning

Determine the thing that can and shall be done, and then we shall find the way.

—Abraham Lincoln

Traditionally, the term *problem solving* has been treated as if it were a single, macrolevel thinking process with set mini procedures applicable to any subject area. Problem solving in mathematics was bundled with problem solving in social sciences, science, language arts, business, and other disciplines. The treatment was a series of steps or procedures that would guide the problem solver from the identification of the problem to the selection of a solution no matter how different the content. Instruction traditionally emphasized similar procedures, followed step by step from problem identification to the final solution.

Although some specific steps might have differed from one expert's method to the next, the variations among models was always slight. A web search of "problem-solving strategies" turns up models that are more alike than different. Note the similarities.

The Eight Steps for Successful Problem Solving: Toyota Business Process

1. Clarify the problem.
2. Break down the problem.
3. Set a target.
4. Analyze the root causes.
5. Develop countermeasures.
6. Implement countermeasures.
7. Evaluate results and processes.

8. Standardize successful improvements. (Toyota Business Process, 2010)

Problem Solving in the Classroom

1. Understand the Problem.
2. Devise a Plan.
3. Carry Out the Plan.
4. Look Back. (Poyla, 1945/2012)

In the emerging century's context and driven by international tests, problem solving is playing an increasingly important role in K–12 education. Two distinct types of problem scenarios are set to overturn old concepts and demand student facility in each. *Tight* or *well structured* problem solving as found in the mathematics standards versus *loose* or *ill-structured* problem solving as found in the social sciences and arts are the focus of PISA's cross-curricular problem solving thrust addressed to nonmathematical problems in social studies, language arts, fine arts, and other similar disciplines. Unlike the good old days when mathematics defined problem solving, problem solving in these other fields has stolen a space under the spotlight.

THE TIGHTLY STRUCTURED PROBLEM SCENARIO

Tightly structured problem solving, such as that advocated by Billstein, Libeskind, and Lott (2010) and others who work with elementary school mathematics, sits at one end of the problem solving see-saw. On the opposite end sit the loosely structured or *messy* approaches such as those outlined in the University of Pittsburg model. The tightly structured approach is most applicable to mathematics and mathematical thinking in science or other fields. The Common Core State Standards in Mathematics note from the outset the importance of students' readiness to "make sense of problems and persevere in solving them" as the first challenge of Mathematics in Practice. Indeed, the verb "solve" predominates the other verbs that initiate the Standards' statements from the 1st grade upward (Introduction, Common Core State Standards in Mathematics, Standards in Practice, n.d., p. 5):

1. Use addition and subtraction within 20 to *solve* word problems involving situations of adding to, taking from, putting together, taking apart, and comparing, with unknowns in all positions, for example, by using objects, drawings, and equations with a symbol for the unknown number to represent the problem (CCSS Standards in Mathematics. 1 OA.A1).
2. *Solve* word problems that call for addition of three whole numbers whose sum is less than or equal to 20, e.g., by using objects, drawings, and equations with a symbol for the unknown number to represent the problem." (CCSS, Standards in Mathematics. 1 OA.A2).

When an early grades teacher is prepared to place sufficient emphasis on mathematical problem solving, students should exit not only having learned to apply skills from this standard, but having acquired the basics of the more rigorous thinking needed to master the tight problem-solving processes in the next grades. Eventually, they will be challenged to apply what they know about problem solving to probability and statistics with its applications to higher math in the workplace and in college.

The Common Core State Standards take a strong position on the primacy of problem-solving instruction in the curriculum. It starts in the 1st-grade standards but certainly does not stop with problem solving in the learning of basic number operations. The standards go beyond deep understanding of math content to challenge teachers to prepare students so they can transfer the application of the operations to increasingly complex problems. Through all the grades, the standards call for first "close" or "near" transfer in the same grade level curriculum to further transfer within the math curriculum and then beyond to eventual "far" transfers in other disciplines and out-of-school situations.

Consider the middle grades standard that ends with the requirement that students *apply* their knowledge about the Pythagorean Theorem:

6. *Explain* a proof of the Pythagorean Theorem and its converse.
7. *Apply* the Pythagorean Theorem to determine unknown side lengths in right triangles in real world and mathematical problems in two and three dimensions.

8. *Apply* the Pythagorean Theorem to find the distance between two points in a coordinate system. (CCSS Mathematics Content, 8.G.B.6-8)

Although a teacher can limit "apply" to workbook examples for numbers 7 and 8 and conclude the literal instruction about the Pythagorean Theorem that fits within a one or two class period time allotment, the teacher determined to end the unit with measureable deeper understanding by all children will not only push the class past completing worksheet examples that have them circle the best explanation (6) or the picture that shows the correct application, but also ask students to measure with real world computer renderings, using hands-on measurement tools such as architects or masons would use and add hands-on tasks assignments to apply the theorem to precise and accurate measurement of a garden wall, a patio, a porch enclosure, a road map, or other similar tasks. With the completion of each, students would make presentations of their work that explain how they figured out and completed the task and how they applied the rule. Of course, included in the assessment of the students' performance would be proof of precise and accurate measurements by the numbers.

Obviously, teaching for deeper understanding will require more time than is allotted in the "old" curriculum and more materials than a text and worksheets. This lesson outlines the increased complexity and suggests that the additional time allotted must increase to result in in-depth coverage of this important concept. When standards call for such thinking actions as "apply," "explain why and how," and especially "find a novel situation," teachers following the standards are pushing students into the types of thinking and problem solving that lead to deeper learning, as evidenced in the transfer for deeper understanding in mathematics:

1. Explain the Pythagorean Theorem and its importance with visual examples.
2. Apply it to produce an irrational spiral.
3. Apply it to find the area of right triangles.
4. Apply it to prove the distributive rule in Geometry.
5. Apply it to check the distributive rule in paper or computer rendered architectural plans of increased complexity or other

real world situations such as a mason, a room designer, or others in similar occupations would face in their daily assignments.

6. Ask students to explain how and why the rule applies in each situation.
7. Ask students to find a novel situation in their town square and apply the rule with a hands-on demonstration that includes hard materials.

When a standard's statement such as "find a novel situation in the town square and apply the rule with a hands-on demonstration that includes hard materials," teachers are asked to promote learning transfer. The Common Core State Standards have placed a premium on the transfer that is most likely to result in deeper understanding through problem solving. In this construct, students learn from doing and reflecting on the problem-solving process, not from completing worksheets or memorizing the formula. To ensure that all elementary students have equitable problem-solving preparation, as early as grade 6, these math standards set the bar high, expecting all students to do and to reflect on their doing so that they can proceed so far as to understand statistical variations and describe distribution practices called for in the upper grade probability and statistics standards (CCSS Mathematics Content, 6 SP 1-5). From there the expectations continue so that middle grade mathematics teachers may devote 75% or more of their time to intentional mediation of the tight mathematical problem-solving processes and ready students for their more rigorous transfer in the secondary mathematics curriculum.

Unfortunately, too many U.S. school districts fall short in two essential dimensions important for success with the expectations set by the standards. First, too many lack qualified teachers ready to teach for this transfer that culminates in mastery of probability and statistics. Second, the current curriculum schedule in most districts does not allow the time for teachers to move students from knowing mathematics to doing mathematics, as called for in the standards. In the present, more coverage is more important than deeper understanding of important concepts (Ben Hur, 2006).

THE LOOSE PROBLEM SCENARIO

Loose problems are described as messy, loosely structured, and ill-defined. Such problems are those found in everyday life and do not lend themselves to an exact set of procedures with set rules of logic followed precise step by precise step. As an example of a loose or ill-structured problem, examine the claims that even developing nations' school systems are outperforming American schools in many dimensions, especially mathematical problem solving and literacy (PISA, 2003, 2009), and that there is clear evidence that students from these nations are taking over allotted seats in American graduate schools.

Students from other nations outperforming American students hurts. Countries once considered "third world" are seating a preponderance of students in American graduate schools. After earning degrees, these students return home to boost their own economies and deepen competition against American companies. Foreign students filling our graduate school seats is a big, messy problem with no clear and ready definition, let alone a quick solution. Opinions on the cause of this problem vary. This variety of opinions place the problem in the loose category in which the tight problem-solving nature of mathematics gives little help.

- Some American educational leaders point to poor K–12 instruction as the problem. They say their states' K–12 schools are doing a bad job. They define "bad job" as "no rigor" or students graduating with high grades, but unprepared for college work and certainly not for graduate school.
- There are political leaders who view the problem in a different way. They see the problem from the view of painfully low graduation rates, persistent low-test performance, high dropout rates, and the achievement gap. They feel trapped by urban teacher unions with large memberships of highly paid veterans who these politicians say drive up the cost of schooling without resulting in higher student performance.
- There are charter school reformers who define the problem as poor discipline, weak financial management, and bad use of traditional teaching methods. These critics describe the pain as a public school teaching force that is tired and out of touch with today's students.

- Steve Zipkes, a principal in a new tech high school holds another point of view. In a blog written for the Partnership for 21st Century Skills, he asked, "Why do educational leadership voices continue to push the very same type of educational structures we have had for the last 100 years, antiquated school buildings, outdated curriculum standards taught in isolation, watered down textbooks, 'sit and get' direct teaching with lecture, lecture, lecture, and an absurd increase in the number of days given each year to testing? More of the same with a little band aid here and there" (Zipkes, 2012).

The variety of viewpoints on the nature of this problem advises the educational community that the national achievement problem is worthy of the messy, ill-defined, or loosely structured label. These terms suggest that many conflicting points of view continue to cloud America's long festering achievement issue.

By their nature, complex, loosely structured problems such as the confusion caused by the decline of American scores on international tests (PISA 2003, 2009) require the careful investigation of many different and often conflicting policies, practices, theories, and pressures. Territories are staked out. Hard problems, filled with affect, advance problem solving into even more difficult terrain with additional subconflicts (Ben Hur, 2006). The fires of emotion stoke attempts to resolve these hard and loose problems, opposing goals, and values pitted one against the other. Peace in the Middle East, terrorism, mind/brain relationships, international piracy, and child slave labor are 21st-century problems that defy easy and clean resolution.

The 2003 PISA tests showed that American students were performing among the average nations in mathematical problem solving. These scores sank lowest with students from urban centers where formal explicit instruction in any kind of problem solving is rare. The 2003 PISA test, however, went a step beyond what most American students were prepared to do. That test, entitled "Problem Solving for Tomorrow's World," included a section to measure 15-year-olds' cross-curricular competencies as problem solvers. It measured what students had learned about making problem-solving decisions outside school walls (PISA, 2003).

Assuming that students would possess basic computer skills such as keyboard use, mouse manipulation, pull down menus, and hyperlinks, two 2012 PISA problem-solving tests measured students' abilities to apply mathematical and cross-curricular problem-solving skills.

It is the cross-curricular, problem-solving test that is most likely to give American students a new set of challenges. In this test, 15-year-olds from 30 nations performed real world problem-solving tasks (e.g., assessing energy needs, trip planning, making a family menu, operating new e-tools without instructions). This test, one that is on the cutting edge of tests and measurements, reflects the curricula of leading countries in achievement such as Canada, Australia, Singapore, and Finland. These countries place a far higher value on developing critical thinking and problem-solving skills both in the classroom and beyond classroom walls than do schools in the United States.

PLAYING CATCH-UP

The U.S. Department of Education has funded two multistate assessment consortia that are designed to help American schools improve their students' problem-solving performances. The consortia are charged to develop a national standardized test that will assess student problem solving and critical thinking performances as well as content knowledge aligned with the Common Core Standards. Forty-eight states are involved. The promise is to measure thinking and problem-solving competencies already buried in these national standards and essential to the new understandings that astute problem solving requires (Note this standard for reading informational text: "Delineate and evaluate the argument and specific claims in a text, assessing whether the reasoning is sound and the evidence is relevant and sufficient; recognize when irrelevant evidence is introduced" (CCCS ELA-Literacy, RI 8.8).

Rather than limit students' problem-solving development to a set of memorized procedures, PISA research shows that the greater emphasis should be placed on critical and creative thinking skills that interact within any problem-solving scenario.

IN SUMMARY

Some teachers have received preservice and inservice preparation to help students, especially the gifted and talented, to learn how to solve mathematical problems and to some extent, more loosely structured problems. In the 21st century, it is important that all students be able to solve a full range of problems and transfer those skills to real world situations. To accomplish this, teachers need the opportunity and the skills to prepare students with those critical and creative thinking skills that are woven through problem-solving scenarios.

Connecting the Dots

- List the three ideas from this chapter that are most meaningful to you.
- Explain why you selected each of these ideas.
- How might you transfer these ideas to your work with 21st-century learners?

A problem is a chance for you to do your best.

—Duke Ellington

CHAPTER 4

Defining Problems: An Essential Prerequisite

If I had an hour to save the world, I would spend 59 minutes defining the problem and one minute finding solutions.

—Albert Einstein

Able problem solvers who can transfer their skills into learning at all times and places are the desired peak performers who will graduate from 21st-century schools. They cannot the exception. They will be the rule.

For teachers in all areas of the curriculum, the first and most fundamental challenge they face in today's classrooms is the development of those students who are adept problem solvers in and out of the classroom. The first skill for these students to master is problem definition. Feuerstein labels problem definition as a crucial *prerequisite* of learning. As such, it is a basic cognitive function that shows up whenever and wherever students are seeking to accomplish a goal with a novel solution (Feuerstein, 1980; Feuerstein, Feuerstein, & Falik, 2010).

All problems benefit from clear definition. Enabling students to develop the cognitive function of problem definition is the starting point for a journey into more mindful, more meaningful, deeper learning. When students have this function intact, teachers can anticipate that their graduates will progress to the point of finding instant and well planned applications for these skills wherever they go in life.

It is essential for teachers to understand that a function is not a set of procedures nor a strategy. It is a way of thinking, a basic habit of mind that is tied to students' motivation. Unfortunately, many texts and websites miss this important point when discussing problem definition. In math, this is especially problematic where information given clouds the fact that as a cognitive function, project definition is an essential determinant of the quality of thinking that students do in the problem-solving process.

In the 21st century, how schools prepare students to be instinctive problem solvers or methodical planners seeking to achieve important goals will be a response to the question of a school's purpose. For those who accept the added role of teachers in these times as developers of students' problem-solving disposition and skills, it is imperative to examine this role as it plays out throughout the curriculum. Why? As noted in the 2012 PISA report on cross-curricular problem solving, the need is for students to learn how to solve problems for both survival and success in the 21st-century work world. That group's definition of problem solving, "Problem solving is a set of activities a problem solver has to invent in order to overcome a problem. The problem is situated in a daily-life situation and unknown. The problem may have more than one unknown possible solution and more than one unknown possible outcome" sets the table for practical ways to prepare students for their unstable world placed throughout the curriculum (PISA, 2012).

When talk turns to discussions of need to intensify problem-solving instruction, it helps to examine what real-life situations look and sound like. In some cases, they resemble the night when, supposedly, Winston Moseley jumped forward to chase Kitty Genovese's attacker on those dark New York streets or the day when bystanders wrestled Sirhan Sirhan to the ground after he shot Robert Kennedy in that Los Angeles hotel kitchen. Or, they may reflect the actions of Navy Seals, such as those sent by President Obama to find Osama bin Laden, who in spite of precise planning and preparation, experienced multiple problem-solving challenges. Or they may recall the decisive thinking of U.S. Airways Captain Chesley "Sully" Sullenberger, who plopped his disabled aircraft down safely in the middle of the Hudson River.

There is no way to predict all the variable problems today's young will face in the complex world of the 21st century. Just as they well know today's world is multicultural and understand that technology doesn't always have control over daily information flow, they will also know that international corporations, perhaps even the ones they work for, live and die in a global economy and that small incidents in tiny countries on the other side of the globe can change how much money they have each day in their own pockets. But with all these global issues over which they may have no control, they will also experience many personnel problems of their own—complex and simple—that will challenge them every day. With adequate preparation, all students should have the level of skill needed to solve problems wherever they may appear on the continuum from simple to complex.

On the *complex* end of the continuum, today's learners will run into problems that are characterized by changing shape and being hard to wrap one's hands around, cloudy with a fuzzy definition, having many variables, and being tough to make sense of which strategies and solutions will work best.

"How do I find a new job?" is a complex question that could hit them at least seven times in a lifetime. They will encounter others: "How often will I have to leave my family to serve in the overseas military?" "Should I look for a second job to support my family?" "Should I move to another state?" "Should I change careers?" "How are we going to take away Dad's driver's license?"

On the *simpler* end of the continuum are problems that have one or two obvious solutions, few paths to a solution, and are well defined with predictable results. The solution hypothesis may come down to "if I do A, B will follow with great predictability": "If I tighten the bike chain, I will be able to ride this weekend. That will make me happy."

Among these simple problems are responses to questions such as "How do I fix this broken shelf?" "How do I keep the tomatoes from freezing?" "How do I trace my lost phone?" "Who gets my vote for school board?" "How much do we have to save for next year's tuition bill?" "What time do I leave for the meeting?" "What do we do about that dead tree on the parkway?"

In whichever way teachers begin an instructional change that will put problem solving at the heart of their students' learning lives, instead of to the side or as an afterthought, they will do well by initiating a transformation to problem definitions within the framework provided by the Common Core Standards.

The identification of select "power" standards, those Common Core Standards that teachers judge are most important for their particular students in a given year, is an important first step. It is these selected standards that can most effectively start the changeover. It is these standards that will form the problem statements that these teachers must address.

After teachers become more skillful making problem definitions based on the power standards, they can increase their own instructional proficiency in creating cross-disciplinary units or projects that prepare students to solve significant and authentic project-based and problem-based learning units. Having experienced the challenge of defining authentic, relevant problems to guide their units of instruction, teachers are more ready to mediate students' skill development, which leads to purposeful development of the students' competency with problem definition.

MEDIATING PROBLEM DEFINITION

Any thoughtful problem definition begins at the back end of the process (McTighe & Wiggins, 2005). Thus, the start is the creation of the final rubric that will guide the evaluation of the proposed definition. Seven mediating questions guide the process and provide benchmarks for assessing the precision and accuracy of the process:

- Is the problem's definition clear?
- Is it precise?
- Is it accurate?
- Does it identify the source of the pain or contention?
- Is it self-contained?
- Is the size manageable?
- Does it create a goal for action?

Clarity. A clear definition identifies a need in readily understandable, jargon-free, and age-appropriate language. The statement of the need or the pain felt is clarified so that those solving the problem can explain the definition in their own words. "Each time I move my neck, a sharp pain shoots upward from my right shoulder to my right ear."

Precision. A precise definition provides exact numbers and terms that are close in value and meaning to the actual measurement that will occur. Precision is especially important in describing tight problems with measurements in mathematics, chemistry, and applied sciences. Of course, detectives want precise reports, as do forensic doctors and accountants. The more the measurement is repeated, the more valid the measurement. A precise answer provides all the details exactly as they are (e.g., "The stick he used to mark the line was six feet long and four inches around" versus "It was a big, thick stick.").

Accuracy. The ability to give a correct explanation that matches exact facts with a high level of accuracy means describing all the details that are present in a situation. Accuracy is especially important in defining loose problems that involve conflict (e.g. "*John Smith and Jane Brown* were the only two people in the red Toyota pick-up" versus "*Some kids* from the north side in a car.").

Source of Pain. The source of pain is an issue causing disagreement, an unmet need or expectation, a disequilibrium, a challenge, or a shortfall. It is a headache that needs an aspirin or more. For teacher teams addressing the Common Core Standards, it can be a simple need such as transposing an ELA standard into a yearlong development task that will teach students how to analyze texts or collaborate in small teams. For students, it may be a problem-based learning scenario focused on making predictions about earthquakes and what product will best show their ability to make estimations.

Self-Contained. A problem definition sets the parameters of the problem. Questions to address include:

- How big is the idea?
- How essential is the challenge?
- What is its context?
- What are the sub-problems?
- What is the focus?

For instance, a middle grade class may decide it wants to solve questions about butterfly migration. They start with the definition of their problem articulated in the question: "Where do all the butterflies go?"

In their initial discussions, they learn how many species of butterflies pass through their town. Given that the project will end in 4 weeks, they decide to limit its scope to Monarch butterflies. Their revised definition reads: "We need to discover where the *Monarchs* that fly through our town go."

Manageable. A manageable definition is one that says: "This is a problem we are confident that we can solve. We have the resources to gather the information, we have a plan for gathering and analyzing the information, we know who will do what for our team, and we know what the teacher wants as the bottom-line end product." The finished definition communicates the team's level of optimism and confidence ("This is what we are sure we can do"), persistence ("This is our plan"), and moderate risk-taking ("This is how we'll Go beyond teacher expectations").

Goal of Action. If the problem definition meets the other criteria, a precise goal should emerge. This goal should bring a solution that the goal makers can achieve in a specific timeframe: "By the end of the week, I will read three chapters."

GUIDANCE FROM THE SIDE

These characteristics of a sound problem definition act as guides for the teacher to use three techniques for mediating student competency as problem "definers": asking questions, giving feedback, and structuring continuous improvement.

1. Questioning to Clarify and Extend Student Thinking. Mediating with questions when students are creating a problem definition removes teachers from being the answer givers in three ways. First, these criteria signal the teacher about which elements are strong or weak in a start-up definition. Second, the questions will guide the students to think about how they will refine their definitions. Third, the questions are encouraging, open-ended, and pushy so that students do the redefining, not the teacher.

Five starter questions help when students are defining a problem:

- How might you rephrase your definition?
- What challenges to your assumptions are important?
- How you will chunk the pieces of your definition?
- What other perspectives might help?
- How can you make your definition more positive and more specific?

Ultimately, a single sentence will capture the problem definition. Modeled first, students can practice within the model as the teacher asks questions that clarify each element of the sentence and makes revisions to their definitions. There are no single right answers to these questions. Each is kept open for the purpose of extending and deepening students' thinking processes.

In this sample, an ill-defined problem starts the conversation: "What can we do about the unbalanced city budget?" The students propose a trial definition. "We need to know what ways the city can increase its revenue each year in order to operate on a balanced budget." Ultimately, after a series of clarifying questions, they refine the statement as a goal to reach. "We need to know three ways that the city manager proposes at least a 15% annual increase in order to operate a budget in which revenues are equal to expenses in all categories."

Using a rubric made from the characteristics (above), the teacher probes with questions: "What are the specific ways you are looking for?" "How soon?" "What do you mean by 'increase'?" "What percentage? What amount?" "What is an example of a balanced budget?" "What criteria determine 'balanced?'" "Can you be more precise about the budget numbers?" "What makes you so sure you can do all of this?"

2. Providing Safety, Encouragement, and Challenging Formative Feedback. Questions that mediate are not questions that intimidate. It is important to ask questions in a tone balanced between encouragement and a challenge to go to the next step. This tone is sometimes helped by preambles such as, "I am going to ask you a pushy question," "I want to deepen your thinking on this definition," "I want to be clear about what you are saying." With these entries, mediators can provide feedback that helps students reform how they are using the problem that is precise and direct without being intimidating. By posing the questions in a positive framework, teachers can encourage students to be tougher on their own modifications. The following questions—from Mrs. Potter, the author's critic teacher during his time as a student teacher at Urbana High School in Illinois— fit well as a lead-in to feedback:

Mrs. Potter's Three Questions

- *What did you do well?* "Let me start by sharing what I think you did well as you redefined your problem statement. I think you found out what you needed to know about the problem and the meaning of words you didn't know. I liked how you predicted what the answer might tell you."
- *What can you improve?* "I think there is some missing information that would make your definition more specific. I am also not sure how you will manage the data."
- *What improvement do I want?* "I would like you to specify the terms I underlined here and I would like you to give me a three-step plan for managing the data. When that is done, I think you will have done a top notch job defining the problem."

3. Strategies for Continuous Improvement. The goal is to improve students' problem-defining competencies so they can construct a well-defined problem statement. Once they have mastered this difficult task with simple and more tightly defined problems, students will need ongoing assistance and support to further develop and refine the defining skills through more difficult lessons and projects. One practice in one lesson stuck in the middle of a semester won't suffice. The more facilitated practice and mediated feedback students receive, the more readily their competency will crystallize and lead to the development of dispositions that will make transfer of the competency easier and more profound. In addition, small, regular, continuous interventions spaced throughout the year are more likely to raise students' feelings of competence as engaged problem solvers.

PRACTICAL STRATEGIES FOR GUIDED PRACTICE OF THE PROCESS

The following strategies will help students practice their definition making skills.

Good News, Bad News. With this advance organizer, teachers can introduce students to ill-structured problem solving. Invite students to take a current relevant problem from the news (e.g., a coming snowstorm, a train crash, school closings). Ask teams to brainstorm the good news and the bad news that this event will bring (e.g., no school, stuck cars). Model how to put the bad news into a problem statement and then ask student teams to replicate your approach before you mediate their trial statements. (Elementary–Middle)

The Best Laid Plans. Invite students to brainstorm a list of interpersonal problems they are having with other students or friends. Make a nameless list. Vote on the top problem, use clarifying questions, and ask students to make it "cleaner" and more tightly defined. After it is more tightly defined, make a goal statement and a three-step action plan to accomplish the goal. At the end of a week, invite students to share progress reports telling where they ran into difficulty. (Elementary–Middle)

Measure for Measure. After students have completed an open-ended mathematics problem-solving unit, build a list of the tactics and strategies used, note which worked best, and construct class posters for later reference on a free Web 2.0 site that provides students with adaptable templates to make posters, brochures, and other print formats (Middle–Secondary)

Now, That *Annoys Me.* Show a word web for all to see. Invite students to share those little things (nonschool) that really annoy them. A problem matrix can help stretch thinking, improve ability to define a problem, and even eliminate it. Start with a matrix as seen in Table 4.1.

Fill in the chart one itch at a time. Complete each entry. Brainstorm solutions to each real problem. Discuss pluses and minuses for eliminating the worst itch. (Middle–Secondary)

The Nine Dots. Connecting dots without mastering this traditional mental challenge (see Figure 4.1) would be like trying to light a lamp without a bulb. To make this problem-solving brainteaser even more challenging, start with the five-line challenge. Once students have mastered this level, try another variation with five or reduce the usable straight lines to four and then three. There is always a better way for this one. End by asking teams to define the problem and compare

TABLE 4.1. Problem Matrix

Itches	Reasons	Bad Results	Real Problem
Whiney brother		Doesn't get way	Lose my temper

FIGURE 4.1. The Nine Dots

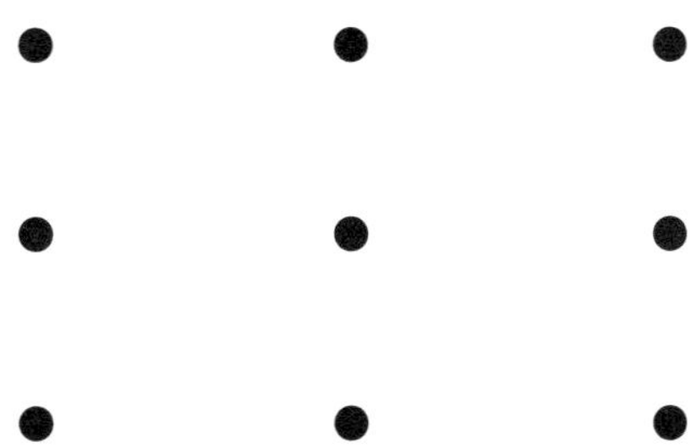

responses. (For the solutions, browse the five-dot problem and be amazed.) (Secondary)

Post It. Place students in teams of three. As a group, students must design an ad for a hard-to-sell product, find experienced eBay sellers (on or offline) that can provide advice or be a doubting Thomas who takes the opposite point of view on the teams' ideas. Students come up with ideas to overcome the objections, make the ad and post it. Note that this assignment begins with a requirement to define the problem. Be sure to mediate the definitions teams make before they proceed. (Middle–Secondary)

The Exit Problem. Most doorways are constructed for daily exit and entry. Occasionally, however, problem situations may arise that call for an emergency exit. The challenge of the exit problem is to find better ways to make exits from tight situations safer. For instance, exit from a plane. What might be better ways for passengers to exit from a large plane on an ordinary landing? In an emergency landing? Think about exits from a skyscraper. Are there better ways for its inhabitants to exit under ordinary circumstances? In an emergency? Invite students to start with an exit that they think is unsafe. Brainstorm alternatives that would improve it. Next, invite teams to combine five of the methods with any five others and create five new ones. Continue this matching task several more times. Delay selecting the best three until they have finished at least three rounds. Discuss the value of this approach in situations the students pick. (Middle–Secondary)

Real World Scenarios. Take an authentic and student-familiar problem (e.g., an unhealthy fast food diet, a habit of being late to class). Describe it in loose terms. Invite student teams to rephrase and define the problem so that it is solvable. Discuss the strategies used to make the problem clean and tight. (Middle–Secondary)

Round Robin Self-Feedback. On a weekly basis, prepare students to give feedback about what they learned about problem definitions. Schedule a 10-minute round robin in which each student in turn completes the prompt "This week about defining a problem, I learned. . . ." Encourage each to build a list of ideas from week to week in an online journal. (Elementary–Middle)

EXPLICIT LESSONS FOR COMPETENCY DEVELOPMENT

Teachers can enhance students' problem definition competencies by planning explicit skill lessons for intentional instruction with seven elements connected in a pattern. This pattern works not only with explicit lessons that promote problem definition, but also with the other critical and creative thinking skills in the problem-solving process. With this pattern promotion, teachers signal the central importance of the process of problem solving in the daily curriculum.

1. Identify The Objective. Share this objective: "To learn how to define problems in our curriculum and apply this to problems in other subject areas and situations." Post it to serve as a reminder to the students that this objective focuses on the process of learning how to think and problem solve.

2. Set the Advance Organizer. Capture students' attention and build on their prior knowledge by structuring literacy tasks (both in literature and informational text) in a problem-solving format aligned with a grade level appropriate ELA Literature standard. After reading age-appropriate stories such as "The Three Billy Goats Gruff," "The Most Dangerous Game," or "The Lottery," begin the lesson with a challenge to define the problem faced by the main character(s). Brainstorm ideas and rank the best options via voting until one is selected. Use this example to introduce a second reading in which you do the same and then let the students know which standard(s) they are addressing and ask them to do a compare and contrast essay.

3. Model a Mental Menu. Present a mental menu as the guide and rubric for refining the problem statement (e.g., "Define"—see below). Use the rubric to assess student progress in defining problems as the start of a lesson:

Describe the character's problem.
Evidence based on description from the text.
Fine-tune the problem statement.
Investigate ways the character would define the problem.
Note additional evidence from the text.
Evaluate that the definition meets the key criteria.

Note that the rubric you create will measure the degree to which students are able to make strong problem definitions. It will focus on the thinking element in the standard.

4. Guide Practice Within a Single Focus. Select another novel, play, biography, or informational text for your grade level and the targeted standard. Use the mental menu to guide students as they define several problems from the story reacting to an essential question about the main character's pain. Focus on the similarity of the pain being experienced in the different works. Examples: *Lord of the Flies:* "What was the precise nature of Jack's, Piggy's, Ralph's, Simon's, and the twins' pain?;" *Letter from a Birmingham Jail*: "What was the precise nature of Dr. King's pain?"

5. Facilitate Cross-Curricular Problem Definitions. Take a step back and assign small groups the task of defining a cross-curricular or real world problem from current events or other situations of interest to the students. Give them latitude to apply the problem definition criteria with as little facilitation a possible (e.g., for primary grades: "Why is there so much fighting on the playground?"; for middle grades: "How can we make sure we all are on time for class?"; for secondary grades: "How is the problem of slavery depicted in U.S. history, American art, and literature?")

6. Mediate Authentic Cross-Curriculum Explorations. Provide students with a cross-curricular problem to define from the view of science, mathematics, and literacy standards. Stand aside, but ask daily mediating questions about problem definition (e.g., "How are you using your analysis skills to identify the challenges of acid rain to our town's environment?")

7. Build Student Reflections on the Competencies. When students are concluding each advance in their development of problem definition skills, insert formative assessments of the "Define" rubric so that they reflect on their learning from doing the tasks (e.g., "When you discussed how to control the size of your problem, what did you learn?," "When you discussed how to make your problem statement more precise, what did you decide to do?," "How are you becoming more adept at finding the evidence you need?")

8. Assess Results. Use the "Define" rubric to assess student definition making, first in the formative stage and then as the final evaluation of the definition skills they have developed.

IN SUMMARY

Albert Einstein's quote at the start of this chapter captures the essence of the paramount role that the competency of problem definition plays in the problem-solving process. ("If I had an hour to save the world, I would spend 59 minutes defining the problem and one minute finding solutions.") Seven criteria provide teachers with benchmarks that will guide students as they use the strategies from this chapter to guide students in understanding the refinement process. Special emphasis is placed on the mediation skills that encourage teachers to work as the guide on the side rather than as the sage on the stage.

Connecting the Dots

- List the three ideas from this chapter that are most meaningful to you.
- Explain why you selected each of these ideas.
- How might you transfer these ideas to your work with 21st century learners?

> *A lot of people in our industry haven't had very diverse experiences. So they don't have enough dots to connect, and they end up with very linear solutions without a broad perspective on the problem. The broader one's understanding of the human experience, the better design we will have.*
>
> —Steve Jobs

CHAPTER 5

The Focus Factor: A Pathway to Mental Engagement

If you chase two rabbits, both will surely escape.

—Unknown

In sports, focus drives a player's intense concentration during a game's crucial encounters. This focus is a mental skill often displayed by great players. Stanley Cup goalie and hockey legend Ken Dryden was one of the first to report how a concentrated focus on the hockey puck made it slow down in his vision (Dryden 1983/2003). Yogi Berra talked about looking so hard at a baseball pitch that he could actually see the stitches turning in slow motion. Downhill ski racers, stock car drivers, tennis players, and pair skaters seeking a coordinated lift know this focus effect.

Top athletes are not alone with this ability. Alexander Graham Bell knew the value of focus in helping him to think through problems he was trying to solve. "The sun's rays do not burn until brought to a focus" (quoted in Marden, 1901/2010) was his analogy to describe the power of concentrated energy that he adopted when he needed to most fully engage his mind with the task. Ralph Waldo Emerson knew how difficult it was to focus his mental attention on what he wanted to say. When writer's block struck him, as he reported it often did, he knew what he had to do to get back his writing power. He had to block every distracting thought out of his mind. "Concentration," he wrote, "is the ability to think about absolutely nothing when it is absolutely necessary" (quoted in Norberg, 2004).

Focus is what enables many restless sleepers to block out distracting thoughts and feelings in order to fall into a sound sleep. Some people focus on how many sheep they can count. Others strive to block any wayward memory, business worry, or distraction by hypnotizing themselves with a repetitious chant: "Sleep. Sleep. Sleep. Sleep. Sleep."

THE FIRST FUNCTION

Concentrated thought or focus is mind over what doesn't or shouldn't matter. It allows the individual to avoid losing the substance of a thought, as Aesop said, "by grasping at shadows." By zeroing in on what does matter, by totally engaging itself to focus on the hockey puck speeding 100 miles per hour at the goalie's head, or the water approaching the fast falling high diver in the midst of a triple twisting somersault, the mind ignores all side distraction with X-ray–like vision. In this way it can control what is most important. Mind over what *doesn't* matter then becomes a laser beam centered on what *does* matter, making every muscle, every neuron and synapse come together as fully engaged, focusing on the mind's singular goal.

Concentrated focus has to stand at the head of the line as the cognitive function that guides all other functions. That is why it is the main title for this book. Focus is the most essential prerequisite cognitive skill necessary for the most effective learning.

Focus is so basic that its cultivation is one that must continue for a lifetime. The novice 1st-grader will use it to concentrate on sounding out new words, building words into sentences, and hearing the author's message. The Nobel scientist will notice how strong her focus is as she peers into a microscope and scans the universe through an electronic telescope. Over and over, as learning challenges increase, this reflective learner asks herself "How well am I focusing?" "How can I sharpen my focus to attend to even more minute details?"

Other examples of focus's primacy as a prerequisite for effectively engaging the mind in the thinking and problem solving that abound in everyday life:

- A child's noticeable increase of focus signals to teachers when impulsive students are learning to control their thinking processes and sustain their attention over longer periods of time.
- When a mother concentrates in childbirth following the doctor's order to "push," she puts all of her mental and physical

energy into the singular goal of using her mind to block out the pain and command her muscles to follow the doctor's order. Just as the mother-to-be's powerful concentration is the factor that enables her to ignore the pain and press the new life out of her womb, focus is the favorable factor that leads to desired results, whether one reaches the goal by will power or aided by a new mini EEG.

- Parents advise young players to "keep your eye on the ball" for a reason. They know intuitively the power of concentration.
- In the workplace, focus enables employees to stay on task. They can learn to block out the phone, ancillary noise from the next cubicle, or cravings for a smoke or drink of water.
- In the classroom, students learn to focus on the teacher's words, the test items they are reading, or the measurement of ingredients for the chemistry experiment.

When standing on the golf course at Augusta with the Master's green jacket a stroke away, when sitting on the Orchestra Hallé stage waiting for a conductor's entry signal, when Green Bay Packers are standing on Lambeau Field waiting for the first ball snap, when standing poised in the Little League batting cage at Williamstown, when measuring minute doses of chemicals in the chemistry lab, the ability to focus counts as much as the skill it takes to finish the task. From focus comes attention to detail. From attention to detail and clear undistracted thinking comes academic success, the putt in the hole, the perfectly played note, or the field goal splitting the uprights.

PRACTICE CAN LEAD TO PERFECT

Getting and keeping a sharp focus, requires a convergence of every bit of mental and emotional energy. Just as focus helps an athlete score a goal or a surgeon make a precise incision, it can help any individual become a better student, develop thinking skills, control emotions, and become a graduate. Success starts from the strength of ability to concentrate on specific tasks and goals, putting the total head and heart into the immediate moment, blocking out distractions, and zealously channeling scattered thoughts and feelings to think about nothing else other than what is necessary to succeed in the task at hand.

Superman was noted for his X-ray vision. Targeting an object, he could use his X-ray vision to see through all but lead. The thickest steel wall could never block what he was searching for. This required him to summon his energy to focus on what he was looking to find.

To apply focus in the manner of Superman, students can train themselves in little and big ways to concentrate on what they want to achieve: a 10.0 triple axel, a flawless speech, a higher course grade, an essay with perfect grammar, or a precise b flat. The sharper their focus on the task at hand, the stronger the concentration, the better the odds of getting what they desire.

Like other cognitive functions, teachers can turn focus to their advantage by teaching students how to increase focus. A first step to sharpened focus is the establishment of the belief that they can sharpen focus. With that belief, practice to make perfect advances students closer to high goal achievement.

THE FOCUS GOAL

Poor thinkers often believe that results of their efforts are accidental. They think good luck is what rains down like manna from the heavens. They believe they have no power to control how they think or act. Some go so far as to think there is no connection between thinking and acting. Oftentimes, only external motivation will get them started.

A University of Pennsylvania sociology study, released in January, 2012, described how students' self-perceptions determined who asked questions in class. On a regular basis, students with at least one college-educated parent raised their hands and asked for teacher help. Students with working class parents with no more than a high school degree were less forward. The latter group did much better after they received coaching from their teachers to seek out help and strengthen their belief in the possibility that they could catch the teacher's attention.

For students who fall in the second "I am powerless" category, a focus plan is a good starting point for discovering how much they can accomplish by taking charge of their thinking. They begin by setting a goal that will guide them to more skillful thinking by increasing their powers of concentration on a specific goal. "By the end of the next 2 weeks, I will double my concentration time." Each day, teachers can encourage these students to start with a 2-minute focus task with instructions like this: "Fix your mind on an object. Concentrate on finding as many details as you can about the object. Write each one down. If your mind strays, start again. Notice what is causing the distraction so you can avoid it. In the first tries, you may stray several times. If you get through the observation within your time limit, stop for the day. Add 30 seconds after each successful day until the end of the 2 weeks. At that time check your goal."

Mary Cabello, a 6th-grade teacher in Illinois, favors focus goal setting at the start of her daily math class. "First, it settles them down. Second, it attunes them to this math class. I want them to make focus a daily habit. Third, it propels them into the focus they need to continue so they are precise and accurate when they are doing their math problem solving. It doesn't take long to make this start up a ritual and a habit."

Dean Hall, a California high school history teacher, subscribes to his role as "focus master." "I teach American History. I favor problem-based learning. We have a double class period. It takes a lot of energy for 11th-graders to keep their minds on the job for 90 minutes, especially in my after lunch classes. I teach my kids to stop and refocus several times a period. Some kids learn to do this on their own. Sometimes, I call for a single group to take time-out so they can put their minds back onto the daily goal."

Susan Ellis, a 3rd-grade special needs teacher in New York, encourages her resource room students to "Catch 40 winks." "A tired mind is a distracted mind, I tell them. 'When you feel droopy, take a power nap. Put your head down and concentrate on putting yourself to sleep by counting down from 100 to 1. Talk yourself to sleep by relaxing one limb at a time. For each limb, count down from 10 to1 with the number followed by a single word such as *relax* or *sleep.* Keep working at it until you fall asleep or the class bell sounds.'"

TAKING TIME WITH TACTICS

In addition to setting a focus goal and taking time-outs to reenergize concentration, there are other tactics teachers can spot through the schedule as teachable moments. Instead of content, focusing is the subject matter.

Chunk It. Teach students to chunk tasks rather than gobble the whole cake in a single bite. To improve students' ability to focus, urge them to emulate downhill ski champion Lindsey Vonn, and practice in small bites. Rather than take a full ride down a new long winding course, Lindsey divides the course into segments and spends one day practicing on each chunk. In this way, she can concentrate on learning the nuances of one section, planning her specific moves to increase her time.

When students are preparing for an exam or planning a project, they can chunk the material and put 100% of their focus on each segment. They plan for no interruptions by turning off the phone, marking the small amount of material to learn, and at the end of the time, testing themselves before a 10-minute break. Chunking also promotes focus when students have to research online information (vary by age starting with 5 minutes as a good time limit), write a paper, read a story, or complete other tasks that tire their minds and draw their attention away from the primary tasks. (All grades)

The Leonardo Clue. "Iron rusts from disuse, stagnant water loses its purity, and in cold weather, becomes frozen, even so does inaction sap the vigor of the mind," wrote Leonardo da Vinci as he expanded his catalog of inventions, paintings, and sketches (Richter, 1888/1970). His colleagues and his rivals marveled at his ability to focus at whichever task was in his talented hand. Today, some admirers mistakenly attribute his daily work of many different tasks to what they called "multitasking." That is a misreading, if not a misinterpretation, of the facts. Da Vinci's detailed notes show that he indeed did complete many tasks in a single day. However, it was one task at a time completed with the ability to block out all interruptions.

Keeping busy was a strategy Leonardo loved as the best way he knew to keep focused on one task at a time while completing complicated tasks such as designing the first submarine or painting history's most famous smile. In this way, this genius gave us a helpful cue: "Help your focus on the task at hand for a set time before switching your attention. Stay on each task on a regular, scheduled basis before moving to something else of interest. Don't multitask. Stop and think." (Intermediate-Secondary)

E-Learning Games. Young children are fans of online games. Go to www.learninggamesforkids.com and select free, age-appropriate learning games that align with your curriculum. Look for games that also develop critical thinking and problem solving. Using the smart board, introduce a sample game that allows you to show students the practice of chunking so they can focus on one task at a time in the game. At the end discuss "stop and think" as a strategy when they get stuck, rather than random guessing. Set up the curricular game so that you can intervene at least once a day to ask, "When did you stop and think?"

ReadWriteThink (www.readwritethink.org) provides many online games that advance the focus agenda while promoting students' academic and problem-solving skills. Select one of these interactive tools to chunk with children: Puzzle Me Words, ABC Match, Word Wizard, Little Blue, and Little Yellow. When mediating children's focus, highlight the phrase "Stop and Think." After each chunk, discuss chunking and how it helps with focus. (Elementary)

Under the Looking Glass. Microscopes, like magnifying glasses, enlarge objects. These looking glasses are tools that provide scientists and detectives with an enlarged view of small objects. They help investigators to focus on specific details they want to examine. Teachers can enhance a student's ability to focus by using microscopes and magnifying glasses to examine an object of interest. As students look through the glass, mediate how they notice special details. Structure students to work in pairs with one student as the "observer" and one as the "recorder." On an index card, the recorder will write a list of the details given. See how many details each pair can gather in 3 minutes without erasing any. Do this once a day for 2 weeks with different high interest objects such as flowers, bugs, patterned materials, and so on. Try to make the lists longer each day. After each session, ask the recorder to note what helped increase the ability to concentrate. At least once a week, guide an all-class discussion that uncovers the different tactics that worked and should be repeated. (Elementary–Middle)

Thread the Needle. Provide each student with a large sewing needle and a piece of thread. See how many times each can thread the needle in a minute. Repeat this task each day for 2 weeks. Each day, show a giant web on the smart board. Ask students to share the focus strategies they used to thread the needle. Take note of what works by asking students to speculate why a strategy worked and record it. (Elementary)

Connect the Dots on a Focus Map. A road map makes a helpful mental guide. Although there are many dots or points on a map, we select those that connect the endpoints of a trip. On a GPS overview,

FIGURE 5.1. A Focus Map

we can see the entire trip from start to finish. A common tactic that helps is to start a trip's plan at the destination of the journey. Perhaps it is grandma's house with rivers and woods to cross; perhaps it is a never-never land so far away that it requires help from others or a special vehicle to get there; or it could be the castle of Oz.

To improve students' ability to focus, invite them to sketch out a simple map (see Figure 5.1). Mark the destination and label it. Pick a task that requires concentration such as writing a required essay or completing a set of geometry problems. Brainstorm the chunks with the class and have pairs or trios select ten chunks that make sense for this task. Plot them as segments on a map. (Go to "inserts" and find clip art. Browse for a map that you can copy and hand out. Also in "shapes" find stars to mark the stopping points and arrows to make highlights). Mark and label the spots and provide allotted times to complete the task. After students finish each segment, they can note on the map what tactics they adopted that were helpful in keeping the focus during that segment. Before they start the next leg, invite them to review what worked and push their minds to do the same thing more intensely, more quickly. Vary the length of the trip by the age of the students. (Elementary–Middle)

Compare and Contrast Map. Comparing and contrasting is the single most repeated thinking skill in the curriculum. It is one of the five critical thinking skills most asked for in the ELA Common Core Standards (Bellanca, Fogarty, & Pete, 2012). In addition, teachers find explicit mention multiple times in K–12 textbooks and assign many compare and contrast essays (e.g., "Write a five paragraph expository essay comparing Hester to her daughter. Quote from the text" or "Tell how each of the three pigs' houses is alike and different").

Note how the compare-contrast competency is required of students directly (compare, alike) and indirectly (distinguish, categorize) in the Common Core English Language Arts strands from the earliest grades. Here are a few examples.

- CCSS.ELA-Literacy.RL.K.9. With prompting and support, compare and contrast the adventures and experiences of characters in familiar stories
- CCSS.ELA-Literacy.RF.K.3d. Distinguish between similarly spelled words by identifying the sounds of the letters that differ
- CCSS.ELA-Literacy.RI.K.9. With prompting and support, identify basic similarities in and differences between two texts on the same topic (e.g., in illustrations, descriptions, or procedures
- CCSS.ELA-Literacy.L.1.5a. Sort words into categories (e.g., colors, clothing) to gain a sense of the concepts the categories represent.

The compare and contrast map presents a rich opportunity to introduce the explicit instruction of this skill set in a stimulating but structured way. It also allows reinforcement of "chunking" student tasks in order to allow practice with focus on one task at a time.

Go to ReadWriteThink (www.readwritethink.org), the free Web 2.0 site provided by the National Council Teachers of English, for many practical interactive tools that promote compare-contrast and other thinking skills. (Classrooms without sufficient technology will find alternative compare and contrast strategies on the RTW site that they can ask students to complete with pen and paper or newsprint and markers.) Set up the task and then give students time in pairs or trios to chunk it. Discuss the strategies they used and the different patterns they developed. Proceed to complete the compare and contrast tasks. End that with their assessments of how chunking helped and where else they could apply the chunking skill in classroom assignments, homework, or family tasks. (Middle)

Focus Games. Games such as Bridge, Rummycube, Gin Rummy, Ping-Pong, and tennis are especially helpful in sharpening focus on a job at hand. For instance, in Rummycube, students must study the board carefully and prepare for several simultaneous moves. As they make moves, they have to block out distractions such as friends talking, noises in the background, and visual movement. They have limited time for a sequence of moves. Set up a game on a Friday after the completion of a unit test. One class period is sufficient. Divide the class into teams of two and set up opposing pairs into a quartet. Once the game has been taught (one class period) a tournament can be set up. Before each engagement in which new pairs compete, put the emphasis on the purpose of the game and tournament: to develop focus skills that enrich problem solving. After each session, allow 10 minutes for the class to brainstorm and discuss successful focus strategies applicable in your classroom.

If students have access to the hardware, select age-appropriate electronic games for the competition. Take the time to have students plan chunking strategies and plot a compare and contrast map with the free electronic Venn graphic maker from Classtools (www.classtools.net). (Elementary–Middle)

E-Timelines. Go the National Museum of American History site (http://americanhistory.si.edu/index.cfm). Search for the timeline builder. Introduce this e-tool to students. Provide a loosely structured problem to set up a timeline for the next unit of history, science, literature, or art. Allow time for teams of three to make a plan for the problem of using the site so they can produce the timeline. During the unit, allow time for the teams to build the timeline. When they are finished, ask each team to self-assess how its plan worked. Focus on how they chunked the task and focused on the events of each period. Invite each team to share what chunking strategies worked best. For following units, repeat the task with an emphasis on students using the best strategies to chunk and focus. (Middle–Secondary)

Why Aren't You Rich? Financial literacy is promoted by the Partnership for 21st Century Skills. This lesson from the American Association for the Advancement of Science (AAAS) (www.sciencenetlinks.com/tools/economics-of-income) provides the basis for a starter economics project with the driving question for a loosely structured problem: "If you are so smart, why aren't you rich?" Structure the problem-solving sequence with a requirement that student teams gather information to answer the question, pose an answer, and make a plan to increase their income. This will require that they chunk the plan from goal forward. In review of the plan, focus on the chunking process and its value in problem solving. (Secondary)

Focus Wiki. Set up a classroom wiki around the question: "What are the best strategies for keeping (select the cognitive function such as focus) on a tough task?" Brainstorm rules for making contributions to answer the question.

Invite all students to make at least one weekly contribution over a month. Allow students to build on other's ideas and highlight the best ones, giving concrete examples. When appropriate, stop for discussion. (Secondary)

FROM TACTICS TO LESSONS

Teachers can interject focus tactics such as those described above in order to build students' awareness of the importance of stopping to think and maintain focus on a task. From short interventions to rich lessons that help students value and internalize the need for focus, teachers can rely on other tools, including questions that mediate and feedback that targets the focus function.

Questions to Mediate Focus. Open-ended mediation that prompts self-evaluation is built on especially powerful mediating questions:

> "How well are you employing the 'stop and think' reminder for yourself or your small team?"
> "How are you chunking this assignment?"
> "How are your focus strategies helping you with this task?" are best asked when teachers catch students racing through tasks. Follow up meditating questions will ask students "what strategies are you using that compel you to stop and think?"

Meditating questions and stems are helpful also as the lead-ins to feedback. Such interventions start when the teacher initiates a feedback opportunity by asking "How well are you doing with ____ in order to keep focus?" or by asking for a completion of a stem "I am improving my focus today because . . . ." When the student(s) have completed their responses, the teacher can "fill in the blanks" with his or her own observations or reinforce what the students said.

Student-Made Plans. The ultimate focus tool that encourages students to reflect on what they are doing, how they are focusing on what they are learning, and how they are intentionally improving concentration is the goal of planning. A look at Feuerstein's list of cognitive functions (Appendix B), will locate *planning behavior* as an advanced support function that enriches all aspects of students' cognitive behavior in whatever discipline.

What is the teacher's role in mediating planning behavior for a cognitive function such as focus? First, it is important that the teacher announces that students must expend effort on developing the function. This includes an exposition of the reasons why this function is beneficial to their thinking and learning. After students engage in a reciprocal conversation in which they recognize the value of concentration and focus, the teacher distributes the plan's outline relying on paper or online options. Next, the teacher walks students through the plan items, explains terms, and answers questions. Third, the teacher monitors use of plans by asking, "What is going well?" and "What help do you need?" and highlighting questions that ask students about focus, chunking, and other strategies they are using.

IN SUMMARY

The focus factor is the most essential of the cognitive functions. It drives students to control their thinking so they can complete increasingly complex thinking tasks. It can direct all of the other cognitive functions so that the thinking being done stays on track. When students think impulsively or episodically, it is difficult for them to maintain the concentration they need to focus their thinking and problem solving. The more complex the content to which they apply their critical thinking skills, the more they can benefit by intentionally focusing on the task. Teachers can help students with planned interventions that call students to attend to the focus factor on a regular basis throughout the school year.

Connecting the Dots

- List the three ideas from this chapter that are most meaningful to you.
- Explain why you selected each of these ideas.
- How might you transfer these ideas to your work with 21st-century learners?

The secret of concentration is the secret of self-discovery. You reach inside yourself to discover your personal resources, and what it takes to match them to the challenge.

—Arnold Palmer

CHAPTER 6

Toward More Systematic Searches

It is best to do things systematically, since we are only human, and disorder is our worst is enemy.

—Hesiod

Many educators are concerned when they hear deficit descriptions of students' abilities, and rightly so. For too many years, such descriptions were turned into destructive labels. Pseudo-scientific labels such as "retarded," "learning disabled," (LD) or "autistic" joined others that lumped individuals in racial, religious, economic, and ethnic categories explained with negative connotations that imposed limits. These categorical limits, often loosely applied, framed expectations that these labeled students could *never* learn: "The class project went well except for our LD students. The special ed consultant told us these kids would never be able to answer open-ended questions. We should give them fill in the blanks worksheets to keep them busy."

Instructional approaches that reinforce low expectations trap these students into low performance. Supposedly, these children's intelligences were limited or they possessed other characteristics that made it impossible for teachers to do little more than fill these students' heads with basic facts or teach them with the least productive methods.

BELIEVING IN CHANGE

In the mid-1950s, much to the dismay of many whose beliefs about the immutability of intelligence were cemented in stone, Reuven Feuerstein postulated the theory that intelligence is plastic and changeable, not fixed for life. Indeed, with the proper mediation of parents and teachers, he hypothesized and gathered data showing that intelligence was plastic and changeable with all learners, including severely challenged children and those with traumatic brain injuries.

In the context of Feuerstein's theory of structural cognitive modifiability (i.e. physical changes in the brain's functions and operations signal increases in the ability to think and problem solve more skillfully), the term "deficient" takes on a new meaning. This theory, reinforced over half a century by research around the globe, not only provided the rationale for a paradigm shift that takes teaching and learning beliefs beyond outdated understandings of what it means to "be smart," but also provides the impetus for new practices and programs that explicitly develop every child's thinking and problem-solving skills. (Feuerstein, Feuerstein, Falik, 2010).

For reasons that are usually environmental and sometimes congenital, a child may have missed the chance to become a more efficient thinker in the earliest years. At home, this inefficient thinking may look like clothes strewn on the floor, toys and books mixed in a random mess, or bikes and scooters scattered unattended on the lawn, all without parent intervention. In school, it may take the form of the disorganized desk jammed with crumpled papers and leftover lunch tidbits or the higgledy-piggledy locker with books, shoes, and who-knows-what-else piled in the bottom that looks and smells like the aftermath of a tsunami. This inefficient thinking is observable when disorganized behavior filters into answers blurted without rhyme or reason, a lack of sequence or order in following common classroom procedures, random guessing without logic, or quickly quitting when faced with a challenging task or open-ended questions.

The good news is that such behaviors do not have to be permanent. These are signs of cognitive deficiencies that are changeable. Proper intervention and high performance expectations that go beyond fixing the immediate situation via punishment or reward (e.g., "You stay in this room until every dress is hung in the closet and every book is back on the shelf . . . and no dinner until it's done") or lowest level task assignments (e.g., "circle one answer" worksheets, fill in the blank answers, "draw a line to the matching term" instructions), help the child break bad mental habits and create a positive mindset that is self-driven, carrying over to become a neat desk, an organized locker, and most important, a mastery of a systematic approach to answer open-ended questions or solve loose problems.

Order and system are but two of the basic ways of thinking that reflect the positive side of the cognitive functions—the efficient functions. Improvement of these functions provides the tools for eradicating the negative and establishing the positive so that students' minds can work without hindrance and perform the cognitive operations that they will need for a lifetime of systematic and effective learning. It may take more time in an intervention with a student who struggles with a systematic approach, but case after case shows that lowering expectations rather than maintaining the high expectations that require systematic problem-solving traps the child in bad habits of the mind.

Feuerstein's studies have identified 26 cognitive functions that respond to well-mediated learning experiences including for those students challenged to learn. He has also developed formal intervention systems to assist teachers in the application of his mediated learning experience theory. Although 99% of students benefit when they have teachers able to mediate their cognitive growth through his systematic programs, teachers without that same intense and formal preparation can still create significant impact (Feuerstein, Feuerstein, & Falik, 2010).

What is the secret? Actually, there isn't one. What some teachers may need to change how students perform consists of no more than abandoning the obsolete belief that children's minds cannot be changed (literally and figuratively) to the understanding that deep changes are possible and desirable. It is then only a question of learning how to. With the addition of Mediated Learning Experience (MLE) skills to their instructional repertoires will come *cognitive* interventions that are intentional, regular, and consistent so that students respond or reciprocate to the high quality teaching that Feuerstein postulated and that recent studies of deep learning reinforce as true, effective, and possible for all students. (Pellegrino & Hilton, 2012).

MEDIATING SYSTEMIC SEARCHES BY ALL STUDENTS

One of the most basic cognitive functions that Feuerstein's theory and practice attends to is the systematic search. In the 21st century, the importance of systemic searching has risen. With the advent of the Internet, the amount of information that impacts daily life has increased a thousand fold. The more information that digital users create, the more the need to sort through, separate, analyze, and distinguish useful information from spam, junk mail, long Google lists with misleading top choices, and other data distractions.

This is even before the student finds one million plus responses to a specific word search and has to wonder how to separate wheat from chaff, bias from actual fact, safety from danger, and distortions from truth. In addition to narrowing the topic, how does the student distinguish relevant and reliable data that will give beneficial information? Systematic searches depend on students skillfully adapting several cognitive functions. In addition to the functions of focus, problem defining, and impulse control, students who master precise and accurate thinking as well as find reasons to support ideas and ask hypothetical "what if" questions are well on the way to developing habitual systematic searches.

Making a Plan. An essential starting point for developing students' systematic search talents is marked when students learn planning behavior. What is this behavior? Think about a time when a friend loses a favorite piece of jewelry, a credit card, the car keys, or an important note. Too often the search becomes a frantic scramble around the house accompanied by swearing and casting blame. The same behavior is evident in the work world when a colleague can't find an e-mail the boss sent to an important client or the budget he had prepared for that special project. The more he fails, the more he blows his top. Alternatively, if he stopped, took a deep breath, and put on a thinking cap to make a plan, he would have a greater chance of finding the object and finding it sooner.

Random and impulsive searching relies on luck. Random guessing and impulsive thinking are cognitive dysfunctions opposite of the systematic search on the continuum. Contrast a random, impulsive guessing game to a search by a system. With a system, the searchers make a mental plan. They might make a map that retraces steps the last time they used the object. They may go looking one room at a time for clues that connect into a pattern. They connect every dot in their mind's eye that they can associate with the object, make a chart, and cross items off one by one. There is order and sequence. The odds of making a bad guess are reduced to a minimum.

Whether looking for that lost ring, trying to find where a cell phone was placed, or locating materials for a work assignment, being systematic in the search pays off big dividends in time. This is true for an old-fashioned search through the newspaper or a digital search with a browser on the computer. With the time saved by a plan, additional time is gained to gather more information.

Gathering Information. Any time it is necessary to look for words, names, places, or topics on the Internet, having a system that guides students in connecting the dots will save them time. It will also lower anxiety and frustration. If they start the search having checked the precise term, exact name, or correct spelling first, they can narrow the items that appear. If they have clarified the group of which the item is a member, students can more quickly eliminate entries that don't fit. Other mental clues such as dates, places, and facts about the item will help cross off items that don't make sense.

Gathering information is the first stage in learning anything new. How well students gather new facts and ideas from other people, books, newspapers, computer databases, movies, Facebook, or Twitter will better prepare them to develop new ideas and solve more complex problems. "As you sow, so you will reap," says the biblical quotation. Students can become more skillful at gathering the most useful information by fine-tuning their brain's search engine to work in an orderly progression.

Systematic searches are more likely to end happily and more quickly when students move with a plan to cover familiar and unfamiliar terrain. They leave nothing to chance. They apply a mental or paper list to make a step-by-step search, retracing their steps one at a time. When they are searching for information to complete a class assignment about Henry Ford, find their mother's best clam chowder recipe, or locate a long lost friend who they think is living in Fresno, the search is more likely to end with a happy result when there is a method to their madness.

SMALL STEPS TO START A SYSTEMIC SEARCH

When making a plan for a systematic search, it helps to include proven tactics and tools that save time, lower frustration, and lead to success. Tactics from this list will develop students' systematic thinking habits as they proceed through the problem-solving process.

Play an Association Game. Wild guesses are a curse when students are trying to find information. More often than not, random guesses waste time. They have enough homework to do without wasting time on blind searches. There are a lot of games that can help students bring order to their searches by initiating explicit instruction about systematic searches. Try Hangman or 20 Questions to wake up short-term memory and put ideas in order. For instance, for a simple task like picking out what clothes to take on a trip, ask "I am thinking about . . . ."

They can also do "What's in a Tweet?" Invite pairs to write a Tweet with a key word embedded about an assigned story they have read. Each team Tweets another assigned pair who must then do the systematic search using the menu in Figure 6.1 as its guide. (Middle)

Organize a List, Check It Twice. Whether students use the old-fashioned index card collection, a sheet of lined paper, a set of sticky notes, or tap into their computer's notes, they may start their search with a checklist. This set of systematic procedures will guide the search.

1. Write out the header, which can be a goal such as "pick college choices" or a task such as "get organic vegetables for this week."
2. Brainstorm ideas, getting as many ideas down as possible the first time.
3. Tuck the list away and come back to it two or three more times, adding other ideas.
4. Group ideas. For importance, rank the items 1, 2, 3, etc. If the list requires ideas to go in a sequence, re-order it from first to last.
5. Finally, make a summary list of the steps taken in order and identify one or two ways to use these procedures to improve systematic thinking. (Elementary–Middle)

Make Delicious Tags. The Delicious Internet site (www.delicious.com) lets students tag or bookmark topics in a very systematic way. They can make knowledge tags, friend tags, revision tags for their projects, or wiki tags. These all help make a fast track connection to a topic or concept with which they are working. To practice start-up tags, stu-

FIGURE 6.1. Browser Search Sequence

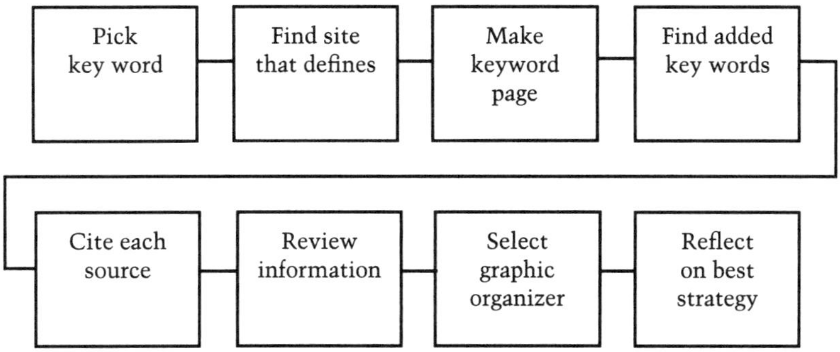

dents can tag friends on Facebook or topics for a research paper. With tagged sites, it is easier to find matching sites of value for a search. (Middle–Secondary)

Show It. Visual organizers can help students think about the order or priority of a task list. Each visual helps organize thoughts in a specific way (e.g., a sequence chart organizes the order of events; a Venn diagram organizes comparisons and contrasts). On a Microsoft Word page look for the "SmartArt" icon under the header "Insert." Students can practice systematic search tactics with one of the SmartArt graphics:

1. Open Word header.
2. Locate "Insert" tab.
3. Open tab and find "SmartArt" icon.
4. Open icon and find diagrams in the Diagram Gallery.
5. Pick diagram type for organizing the search.
6. Complete the diagram with information gathered.
7. Reflect on how these procedures help with a *systematic* search.

After students open the diagram gallery, they will see six organizers. Each can pick the organizer that works for the type of thinking they want to do.

- *Target:* Pinpoint what is the most important idea (at the center) to the least important (outside ring).
- *Triangle:* Show priority: most important idea or fact (top) to least important (bottom).
- *Circle Sequence.* Add number and additional small circles to connect ideas in order from first to last.
- *Organizational:* Main ideas with sub-ideas below.
- *Web:* Brainstorm a lot of ideas in order of preference from right to left.
- *Venn:* Compare ideas that overlap around a key point. (Middle)

What's the Big Idea? Pick any task students will have to do in the next week (e.g., write a report, read a short story, complete a word problem set, deliver a pizza, complete a lab experiment, etc.) Ask the students to think systematically about the task by answering these questions: "Why am I going to do this?" "What is my step-by-step plan of action?" "How will I know I did it systematically?" "What have I learned about being systematic?" "Where can I use the insights I have gained?" (Middle–Secondary)

Make a Dots-in-Order Chart. On a large notepad for the whole class to see, lay out a series of dots across the page about one half inch apart. Below each dot make smaller dots dropping from each of the larger dots. Keep them a quarter inch apart and connect with a line. On the larger dots, write the students' tasks for a day such as do dishes, clean bedroom, do homework, eat breakfast, etc. (see Figure 6.2). Invite the students to arrange the dots in time order before taking each task and thinking about the steps to get the first job done [e.g., (1) clear the table, (2) load the dishwasher, and (3) add soap]. Repeat this for the other jobs (this may require several days with young children). Discuss with the students the value of this step-by-step system and ask them how it might work with other daily tasks. Following this with a systematic restructuring of a week's or month's tasks helps to strengthen orderly thinking by being explicit in bridging what they have learned. (Elementary)

Finders Keepers. When a person loses a favorite pin or misplaces a cell phone, she knows the best way to find it is to retrace her steps in

FIGURE 6.2. Sample Dot Chart

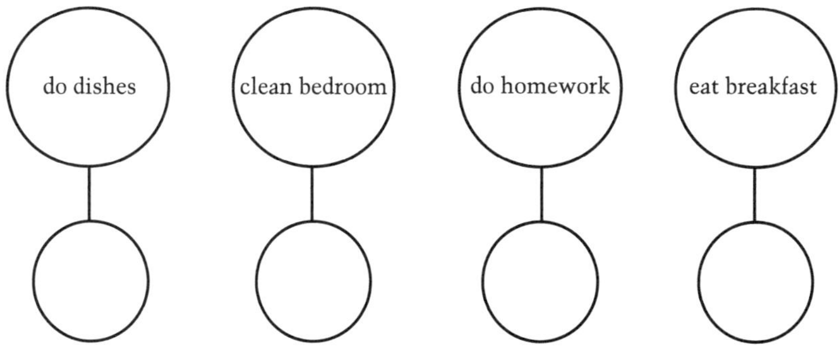

a systematic way. Use lost item searches as an advanced organizer for the development of students' systematic search skills. Create a poster with the steps shown in bold (see http://edu.glogster.com). Discuss the steps with the class before having pairs hide an item in the classroom and inviting another pair to practice the procedures. Start step one with a pair-to-pair interview. End with a discussion of the rationale for doing a systematic search.

1. *Write out a list.* Identify where you were since the last time you remember having the object.
2. *Put the items in reverse order.* Proceed from the most recent to most far back.
3. *Go back to each location.* Stop and look around in a clockwise motion. Each time you notice a specific spot where you might have put the object, go to it.
4. *Use a system to look.* For instance, you may select a desk. Start with the top, then go to the right hand drawers in order, and so forth.
5. *Keep the same pattern.* Repeat each spot's search in the same way (e.g., top to bottom). (Elementary–Middle)

File and Code. On and off the computer, creating files to track what students read or to save journal entries on completed tasks is worth the time it takes. Before students start a systematic search for information, they have to know what they are looking for. For each key idea, students can make a new file folder and label it. Make sure they code the files so that the files appear in the appropriate storage section (e.g., My Documents, My Desktop). For codes, insist that they use a name, initials, or numbers that connect to the main question they are investigating. Thus, when they go to retrieve the documents, the key items will all pop out.

At the start of the unit, prepare an explicit lesson that walks students through this file-making process. For the unit, stop the lesson each time you want them to make a file entry. Provide a checklist and encourage paired partners to check each other's work. At the end of each checkup, discuss issues and give formative feedback. At the end of this explicit facilitated practice, summarize key points learned about making the folder. In future units, repeat the process. (Secondary)

Review It. After students have finished one or two topic searches and have set up a folder system, take half a class period for them to assess what they have learned about being systematic with their searches. How did they go about the search? How systematic was it? How could they save more time by being more systematic? What would you do? To help them gather more ideas on how to search systematically, encourage them to browse the term "Internet searches." This should lead them to lists of tips for Internet searches. Open and preview at least three before picking the ones they like best. Make a master list and save it in a documents file for review and checkup. Make a checklist that you can use as they practice being systematic in all searches. (Secondary)

Puzzle Possibilities. Ask students about a puzzle they have had to solve at home or in school. For the youngest children, show a simple familiar map puzzle (e.g., The United States). Give them an outline of the map and invite them to break the map into sections. If they sketch the puzzle outline they can then follow these steps to guide them in putting the pieces together. Post these steps on a bulletin board for easy reference.

1. Look at the box. See the big picture.
2. Look for all pieces with a straight edge.
3. Match the images on the edge piece to the big picture on the

box. Put the straight edges into four piles that reflect the four edges.
4. Match the scene pieces as closely as possible on each edge.
5. Select other pieces by color and detail to fit inside the edge pieces. Look first for shapes that fit the shape of the outside pieces.
6. Continue to the inside.
7. Discuss what was hard and easy. (Elementary)

People Treasure Hunt. Treasure hunters can be haphazard in their searches. Winners, however, are systematic. As an engaging advance organizer for the concept of systematic searches, start the explicit skill development lesson with a treasure hunt. First, prepare a list of interesting, positive tidbits about each student in the class: "This is a student who . . . ." Put the students into search teams of three. Instruct them to organize the search so they can be the first done. They are allowed to get one clue from each student, but students may not give their identity away. Students must give the same clue to everyone who asks. Instruct each team to plan its search strategy. At the end of a set time or when a team identifies all, hold a class discussion to identify successes, missteps, and tragic choices in the search plans. Make a list of what worked best before discussing its applicability to systematic searches and leading to inquiry lessons or projects. (Middle–Secondary)

MESSY PROBLEMS AND SYSTEMATIC SEARCHES

Students' reflections on systematic thinking can help teachers decide the extent of explicit or implicit development of this important cognitive function. There can be little doubt that systematic thinkers hold an advantage that benefits their gathering and making sense of the curriculum, especially if it is organized on a cross-curricular problem-solving approach. That was true well before the digital age.

The PISA 2012 assessments contain two frameworks devoted to problem solving. One focuses on solving mathematical problems and the other on cross-cultural and real world problems (PISA, 2012). In the document that outlines the plan for these assessments, distinctions are made between ill-defined, loose problems and well-defined, tight problems. The following activities focus on systematic searches for solving messy problems.

Amazing Mazes. The Internet is filled with sites that provide interactive mazes that teachers can transform into age-appropriate opportunities to develop the systematic search function in a problem-solving format (e.g., www.clickmazes.com). Follow these steps with a sample maze. After students see what is expected, use the variety of mazes to differentiate systematic problem-solving practice.

1. Show the puzzle.
2. Ask student's "What's the problem?" ("To complete the maze").
3. Brainstorm strategies to solve this problem. ("What do you have to do?") Sequence the procedures from the brainstorm.
4. Brainstorm stuck strategies. ("What do you do when you don't know what to do?") List these ideas for all to see.
5. Select the mazes instructing students to follow the ideas brainstormed.
6. When students have finished a maze, instruct them to write: "What I did well to solve this problem in an orderly way" and/or, "What help I needed."
7. Adjust levels of difficulty for each student's selection of the next maze.
8. Select times to discuss the question, "How are these mazes helping me become a more systematic problem solver?" (Upper Elementary–Middle)

Paired Partners Solve Messy Problems. Providing students in the middle and secondary grades with opportunities to apply what they are learning about systematic searches will give students much needed experience with solving loosely defined problems.

1. Prior to sharing with students any model menus for problem solving, present this loosely defined challenge showcasing the need for being systematic in searching for a solution. Use a think-pair-share format that invites each student to think

about this messy problem statement: "You have solved many problems in your life. Think about what the word 'problem' means to you. Then think about some examples that you solved. How did you solve the problem? What steps did you take?"

2. Allow 3 to 5 minutes. Students may jot down their ideas before you match them in pairs. In the pairs, they should agree on the definition and each pick a good example.
3. On the smart board, begin a project web. In the center, write the word "problem." Ask pairs to contribute their definitions. Without duplicating, add to their ideas with examples. In the end, summarize what they have said.
4. Add a second web on the second day. Repeat the think-pair-share process using the word "systematic." Ask the questions and encourage pairs to agree on terms and examples before posting on the web. The key questions: "What does the word *systematic* mean?" and, "What examples can you recall of your own systematic problem solving?"
5. On the third day, invite the pairs to discuss and share the benefits of systematic problem solving.
6. At the conclusion of the third think-pair-share, invite several students to build a summary of the key ideas before asking each student to make a journal entry with his or her own summary. Coach the summary making as needed. At later times during the semester, invite students to make additions to the summaries. (Middle–Secondary)

IN SUMMARY

Random and haphazard or orderly and systematic? That is the challenge 21st-century students face in this information saturated era. Students can learn how to be systematic as they search for information. Students can approach each information search with many of the same digital tools that often add information to the saturation. These tools guide the step-by-step search, eliminate random jumping about, and encourage students to think in patterns rather than with random guesses.

Connecting the Dots

- List the three ideas from this chapter that are most meaningful to you.
- Explain why you selected each of these ideas.
- How might you transfer these ideas to your work with 21st-century learners?

It is astonishing what an effort it seems to be for many people to put their brains definitely and systematically to work.

—Thomas Edison

CHAPTER 7

Asking Productive Questions

Millions saw the apple fall, but Newton was the one who asked why.

—Bernard Baruch

Whenever teachers have made higher order questions and higher order objectives central to their teaching, their students have performed at higher levels of achievement (Marzano Research Lab, 2012). With Bloom's taxonomy as their guide, the most demanding of teachers have raised their expectations of students and signaled that analysis, synthesis, comparisons, proofs, and other "high order" mental operations now enumerated throughout the Common Core State Standards would drive instruction. From questions that asked, "What's the connection between . . . ?," "What would happen if . . .?," and, "What's the difference between...?," to essay topics that commanded, "Compare . . . ," "Explain why . . . ," "Defend . . . ," and, "Prove...," to graphic organizers that asked students to identify attributes, show cause and effect, or predict outcomes, complex thinking from Bloom's higher levels drove these teachers' daily instruction. Intuitively these high performing teachers knew they didn't have to worry about achievement scores. They worried more about how to make sure their students *understood* the course content and could make use of complex cognitive skills needed for advanced education and multiple careers in an increasingly complex work world. Such was their contribution to the concept now called deeper learning (Pellegrino & Hilton, 2012).

In our information-overload age, asking the productive question is proving to be a much desired commodity that helps students refine their online and offline problem-definition and systematic searches. Asking the right productive question signals students' abilities to seek results-aligned answers about important issues and problems that they are investigating. From many points of view, *not* asking productive questions is a deficient cognitive function, as well as a major hindrance to the development of student inquiry and mastery of the content.

In the real world outside classroom walls, failure to ask a doctor "why?" about a recommended surgery could lead to a patient with more complications than cures. Failure to ask teens where they are going late on a Saturday night or what they are doing on the Internet could lead to dangerous liaisons. Put off asking how the family car's front fender was dented and a parent is likely to miss clues to some family member's wild driving.

Practical issues are a miniscule piece of the worldwide information explosion. A video article, *The Explosion* of *Data*, claims that every 5 minutes, an explosion of digital data equivalent to all of the information stored in the Library of Congress occurs (see: inside-big-data.com/video-the-coming-explosion). Eric Schmidt, former CEO of Google, asserts that in this decade as much information is created in 2 days as was generated from the dawn of man through 2003 (Coyle, 2013). Almost daily, CNN sprouts instant pictures of atrocities in countries most cannot name. Instant messages on smart phones describe cataclysmic tragedies before the first broadcast news alerts. Newscasters cast aspersions and make biased pronouncements about political fault before national leaders receive the first briefing of the day. Skyscrapers fall before our eyes. Tsunamis wipe out lives as our children sit thousands of miles away helplessly watching death and destruction. Teens sneak peeks at pornography sites disguised as legitimate businesses.

Some would argue that the best way to help students survive this 21st-century information storm is to increase protective laws, close down Internet sites, and strengthen bans on pornographic sites. Indeed, the lists of Internet sites helpful for parental information control is long. The range of tools, advice blogs, and tutorials is impressive. However, as fast as a novel parent control, web 2.0 tool, blog, or advocacy site comes online, a new advance in technology subverts it. And even if there is not a new subversive tool, it is likely that young people in an ever more tech-savvy generation find ways to break parental locks. Short of chaining children in their bedroom closets and dropping the key in a bottle of acid, what is a parent to do?

BAD NEWS, GOOD NEWS

The bad news is that never in history has it been more necessary for parents to feel that their children are safe. Never has there been a time when the education of our youngest, especially with the skills needed to control information, has been more necessary. "My son would live on the Internet. He is just 7 with the computer skill of a high-tech wunderkind. This sounds great, but his judgment doesn't match his attraction. If he could he would have unfettered access. Now, our best ball and chain is to change passwords daily on all of our computers and spend lots of time pointing out why some sites are out of bounds," (Private parent conversation with the author, 2012).

The good news is that educators' understanding of how to leverage explicit instruction of the complex thinking skills, including how to ask productive questions, will empower young people to control the technology world around them. As in times past, the best answers are in the hands of teachers prepared to teach these needed skills not only to the young people, but to their increasingly desperate parents

Formal, explicit instruction in robust questioning skills is a key step for empowering young people to control the information explosion. Built on skills for making systematic searches, questioning skills can provide three unique advantages never before needed, at least to such degree, for students to take charge of the information that bombards them willy-nilly every day.

The Control Advantage. When the 2011 tsunami wracked northern Japan, the giant automaker Toyota was all but destroyed. However, within one year, its factories were operating at full capacity as the world's largest car producer. Although it would be nice to think that schools could make a similar recovery from the 21st century's information tsunami, economics prevent any such revival. That is not to assert that the school community cannot make sufficient, significant changes to help parents and teachers better prepare young people to control and survive the information floods, but the ever changing information storm makes the solutions more elusive.

The Common Core Standards provide a starter kit for this endeavor. If coupled with performance assessments, ones that determine how well students can solve problems using the thinking skills embedded in the standards and transfer applications of these skills outside the school curriculum, these two tools, the standards and the assessments, will expand students' survival kits.

Consider the possible positive effects of a K–12 school curriculum that dedicates 1 hour a month intentionally to develop students' questioning skills. By the end of the primary grades, young children would have reinforced their natural "why?" questions; by the end of middle grades, pre-adolescents would have developed the disposition for skepticism of misleading and biased informational texts and broadcasts, becoming able doubters about text messages, Tweets, Facebook accounts, bogus news reports, and pre-teen rumor mongering. Knowing that their children were proficient with mindful tools for controlling thoughtful acceptance or rejection of what they saw or heard via the news media, or competent in their questioning skills to analyze for bias or play devil's advocate of online messages, many parents could rest easier knowing that their children had a control advantage.

The Understanding Advantage. Not long after the start of the 21st century, voices began to express concern about the regurgitation curriculum inherited from the 20th century. The twenty-first–century skills movement, propelled by America's less than shining results in international competitions (PISA, 2009) was initiated by articles written by world-class corporate executives such as Boeing Aerospace's and Deloitte & Touche's CEOs (Stewart, 2006) along with studies by the American College Testing Service (2012), and multiple professional education organizations such as ASCD, NEA, and the Council of Chief State School Officers. All pressed for deep revisions, even a major paradigm shift, in the content and methodologies that had driven instruction into a one-sided, extreme emphasis on increased standardized scores. A principle source of contention was a curriculum being driven by these low-level assessments and the No Child Left Behind Act, prompting schools to rely on the memorization of measurable facts in order to avoid sanctions. The not-so-subtle threats that came through state education departments were perceived as pushing schools mindlessly toward a single intimidating annual achievement goal: the notorious Annual Yearly Progress (AYP) standard. The second, but equally grave concern centered on the content of the curriculum itself. As pointed out by the conference board and the Partnership for 21st Century Skills (2012), the 19th-century–like curriculum with its narrow and obsolete focus on facts was in need of a drastic 21st-century revision. Their suggestions included new literacies to develop students' understandings for careers in the finance, media, information, health, environment, and technology disciplines, as well as new methodologies and new assessment tools that would return the rigor of significant and relevant understanding of concepts to the classroom.

The term "understanding" is defined as the ability to grasp meaning. Deep understanding grasps deeper meanings. Meaning sits on a see-saw balanced on one end by the literal information that is the bones of the curriculum and on the other end with the figurative interpretations that are the blood. Together these two ends connect the flesh or meat of a concept. Complex concepts and big ideas require a balanced examination of all the elements that can be deepened as new information and new interpretations flesh out the concept and provide greater insight or understanding.

Questioning is a basic thinking skill that students must improve in order to deepen their understanding about a concept. Questioning becomes productive when it gives them the skills to manage information, solve problems, and enhance how they learn. Of course, when students are presented with the barest facts to describe an object, they need only recall what they are told. "Our car is a red, two-door Ford Focus sedan with the license plate Illinois 123. The front bumper is missing." If they have to dig deeper beyond the facts to put more pieces of a puzzle in place as they do with abstract concepts, then they need to ask questions that will not only gather additional factual information, but analyze, compare, draw inferences, compare parts, make connections, sequence, determine cause and effect, and select other complex mental operations. "I'm not sure on what floor of the parking garage I left the car, but I can try to give you some clues. . . ."

Simple tasting, seeing, hearing, and touching will not satisfy an inquiry for a concept's often hidden and complicated abstract meaning. Love is more than a matter of holding hands. Peace is more than a matter of a signed piece of paper. To activate the necessary cognitive operations for discovering complex meanings of love, peace, and other abstract ideas, students have to ask the appropriate questions so they discover the multifaceted nuances that are often hidden from the senses. "What music did you hear when you left the level on which you parked the car?" "Was the ramp going down or up?" "Was there a color code?" are questions that may solve the mystery of the lost car. They are, of course, easy in comparison to the many attempts in literature, psychology, history, and other disciplines to define the complexities of love and peace.

The more able students are to ask the right questions, the precise questions that will result in clues coming together to make sense, the more they are able to understand what they need to know. The more skillful students become in asking questions about hidden meaning, the better they can gather the information needed and apply the thinking skills that will give them the understanding advantage.

The Achievement Advantage. What happens when a teacher prepares students to understand that "the right question" is the one that is a *productive* question? What happens when teachers prepare students to ask productive questions that end with significant and relevant results? Compare these two examples:

> Sophie, an AP English student, is puzzled by her assignment: "Compare a major character from Wuthering Heights with a character of your selection from any current TV drama." She knew that the rubric for her paper was based on an ELA standard:
>
> • "Analyze the impact of the author's choices regarding how to develop and relate elements of a story or drama (e.g., where a story is set, how the action is ordered, how the characters are introduced and developed)" (CCSS.ELA-Literacy.RL.11-12.3).
>
> Sophie's teacher, Mrs. Paulson, had presented that standard at the start of the unit. In fact, the class had spent 3 days comparing Catherine and Heathcliff. Mrs. Paulson had given a wonderful lecture showing a detailed Venn diagram about the lovers' similarities and differences. She had even illustrated it with video clips from the novel's various movie versions. The class had spent a whole day listening to their teacher point out the fine differences in Heathcliff's speeches. Sophie's favorite was Laurence Olivier's interpretation.
>
> But now, Sophie was stumped. Mrs. Paulson hadn't used any examples to compare TV shows. Not a one. Sophie had kept her usual meticulous notes. Where should she start? How was she ever going to write this paper? What did the teacher expect?
>
> Roger, a senior English student in an average track, wished Mr. Stark would lecture just for once. Instead, it was Mr. Stark asking question after question. The teacher had started the first unit

of the year with a big question he called "my driving question." Now that it was the second quarter, Roger had the pattern nailed. He knew Mr. Stark would start their book study, this time it was Shakespeare's *Othello* and Mamet's *Race,* with a guiding question that was tied to a new standard. Sure enough, the question provided a huge challenge. "How do movie producers' interpretations of the texts result in creating characters that reflect or differ from what you think is the writer's intent?" Roger was able to match the question with a standard that the teacher posted for all to see: "RL.11-12.7. Analyze multiple interpretations of a story, drama, or poem (e.g., recorded or live production of a play or recorded novel or poetry), evaluating how each version interprets the source text. Include at least one play by Shakespeare and one play by an American dramatist)."

Outside class, Netflix gave Roger and his friends a chance to watch Orson Welles interpret *Othello.* After reading the plays, they had taken a field trip into Chicago to see the Goodman Theatre matinee production of *Race.* Roger and his group were assigned to develop a list of guiding questions they had about what they had read and seen. Mr. Stark modeled the types of questions, posted a copy of the "Three-Story Intellect" (Fogarty & Pete, 2005) and had checked in on their discussions and the questions they were going to ask. The whole class had discussed the most pressing questions nominated by each group until they winnowed the questions down to five for each play.

To cap their inquiry, each team would design a web page representing their interpretations.

Roger smiled. The web page business didn't faze him. Sure, it was harder than writing another essay like he had done with the last book. This time, Roger would have to work with a group. He thought it would be more fun. The questioning model Mr. Stark had laid out made Roger confident that he could ask questions that got to the soul of the assignment. With a structure to guide his inquiry and focus on the information he needed to highlight, he was ready to work with his team.

When students learn how to ask productive questions, as Roger and his classmates did, they enjoy the achievement advantage, even over the AP students who were reduced to taking notes from a lecture. Productive questioning is a standards-aligned 21st-century critical thinking skill, one that enables students to gather and analyze the information that they will need to know and do in order to be college ready (Conley, 2007). In addition, explicit instruction in how to ask guiding, probing, and clarifying questions, provides students with a learning tool that promotes insight into significant problems as well as test questions. By learning to understand the practical difference between analysis, synthesis, and other key words that describe a specific type of critical thinking, Roger and his classmates have increased their fluency by building a vocabulary of key words that direct them to precise cognitive competencies. Being asked to develop complex questions that promote complex thinking is the heart and soul of robust and rigorous academic inquiry. Students with K–12 learning experiences in which teachers regularly, consistently, and explicitly prepare them to ask complex questions about rich content with systematic, intentional, and complex lessons about analyzing, proving, distinguishing, and comparing, will be most ready with a stronger set of learning skills.

THE STANDARDS SPEAK

As early as grade 1, the English Language Arts Common Core State Standards call for students to know how to ask questions. (CCSS.ELA-Literacy.RL.1.1: "Ask and answer questions about key details in the text.") Each year after, the ELA standards up the ante. When helping students turn into productive questioners, learning to ask factual questions is an important ingredient for advancing students' literacy skills. From the earliest years, student-asked questions are the alpha, but not the omega. The first, 1st-grade reading questions focus on gathering concrete data: "What is this?," "Who did that?," "When did this happen?," "Where did that happen?," and "What are the events?" They are questions that guide young students to uncover the important facts and know how to find the information they need. By grade 4, that literacy standard has evolved to ask that students "refer to details and examples in a text when explaining what the text says explicitly and when drawing inferences from the text" (CCSS.ELA-Literacy RL.4.1). To develop this skill it helps for students to add clarifying questions (e.g., "What are your text examples?") and probing questions (e.g.,

"Why do you think that?" What clues can you provide to back your claim?" "What is your evidence?").

Essential Questions. To transform students into skillful questioners of ideas and concepts, teachers need not take giant steps. They do not have to make oversized, time-gobbling changes to answer the question, "Where do I start?" They only need to think of any lesson in a standards-aligned curriculum from the perspective of "students asking" rather than "teachers telling." For this, a well-formed and precise lesson on "essential questions" can start the changeover. The essential question habit will replace obsolete goal statements for initiating a lesson, project, or unit. Instead of a low level goal that states "students will recall . . . ," teachers getting ready to stimulate student questioning begin a lesson that will keep students' eyes glued on the starter question that best springs from the students' point of view, interest, or experience.

The most important point that teachers must keep in mind when they frame an essential question is that it should not have students dwell on facts. Open-ended, the question should motivate student interest by asking them to consider the topic or issue with as creative an answer that they can imagine. In a blog post, author John Mergendoller notes that a strong essential question will never lead to answers findable on Google or any other search engine. Google does the facts. The students' essential question should lead them to deeper understandings. (Mergendoller, 2012).

By spotlighting their own essential questions that ask students to probe deeply into curriculum content, teachers model the quality of questioning that will most help students investigate a problem. The open-ended model will also lead students away from any expectation of superficial factual recall and into the depths of rich understanding of complex, "big" ideas.

The following are samples from teachers with experience as *essential* question-askers that meet the criteria:

- "How do students from different countries show the ways different from our ways that children in those countries travel?" (Elementary, Wauwatosa School, Wisconsin and Buna Tce School, Australia)

- "From what participants in the Civil Rights Movement tell us, how do we think small acts of courage changed society in America?" (Middle Grades, King Middle School, Maine)
- "What does safe driving mean in the world of physics?" (Secondary, Codman Academy, Massachusetts)
- "How do we think a search for scientific facts might create engaged, active, and accurate field-guide writing about our local vernal pool?" (Elementary, Four Rivers Charter School, Massachusetts)
- "How can we use our math skills to reconcile decisions about local land use management?" (Secondary. City Arts and Tech High School, California)
- "Am I my brothers' or sisters' keeper?" (Secondary, City and Arts Tech High, California)
- "California, Who Are You? How do we think geological and environmental issues affect our lives in California?" (Secondary, City and Arts Tech High School, California)
- "If we migrated to Mars, how would we survive?" (Middle School, West Ed. Regional Laboratory, Oregon)
- "What lessons do senior citizens have to teach us about the history of our community? (Elementary, Foxfire, North Carolina)
- "What explorers belong in our state's Hall of Fame?" (Elementary, Sherwood School, Highland Park, Illinois)

After students become familiar with modeled key words in essential questions that stimulate open-ended problem solving and novel solutions, teachers can initiate the transfer process. By showing a chart, such as Fogarty and Pete's "Three-Story Intellect" (2005), teachers can assist student teams in framing their own essential questions (see Figure 7.1).

Asking Guiding Questions. The second type of questions that teachers can ask the teams to develop are called "guiding questions" (Denver Green School, 2012). These are questions that guide an investigation through information found on a site or in an informative article. For instance, in Phase 1 of an ELA standards 1st-grade-aligned project about "amazing whales," a 1st-grade teacher in Columbus, Ohio, start-

FIGURE 7.1. Three-Story Intellect (Fogarty & Pete, 2005)

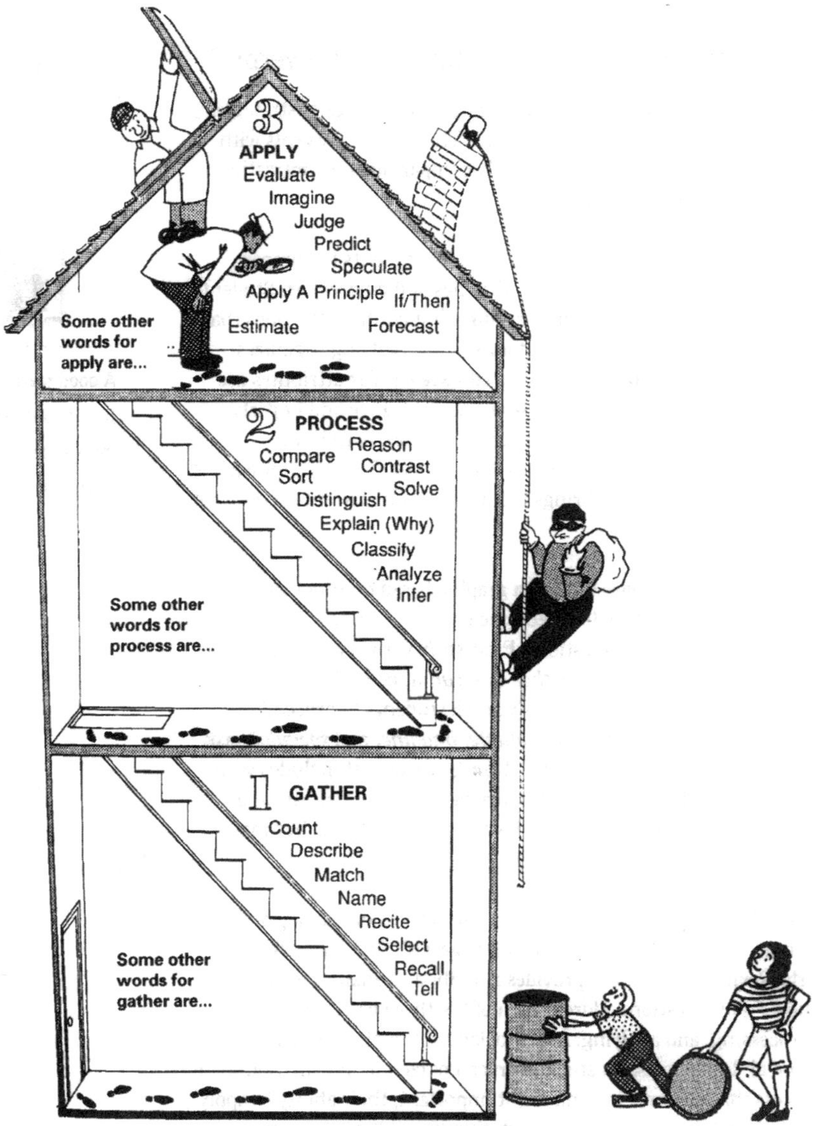

ed with the essential question, "In how many ways are the whales in our book like each other?" After displaying a matrix on her smart board, she entered the names of each whale mentioned in the first column. When a student volunteered an answer to the essential question, she wrote the response as a column header. "They are the same color" (color). "They have big eyes" (size). After she filled the column, she asked the students for facts. "What color is your whale?" "Are its eyes big?" After all have answered, she asked if the header statement was true or false and pushed for the reason why or why not. She closed the discussion by asking the students, "What have you learned about asking good questions today?" and wrote their responses on the bulletin board. On the next day, she reviewed these responses before she continued her emphasis on helping the students learn how to ask questions. Her colleagues teased her by alluding to the Chinese proverb, "She knows how to teach her students to catch fish, not just eat them."

When teachers teach students to build their own guiding questions, teachers raise the ante from a lesson that presents information to be memorized and practiced on worksheets to a lesson that asks students to search for information for themselves, gathering data just as researchers would, understanding differences among variables, being assessed both on the new information acquired and on their deeper understandings about how two ideas or objects are different and on how they are asking more complex questions.

Bill Gregory and Vernoy Johnson, two master teachers in New Trier High School's Center for Self Directed Learning, an alternative school-within-a school (1972–1982), are remembered by their English and math students for what one student (now a professor at the University of Pennsylvania who researches addiction among veterans) calls

> their maddening propensity to start the year with ground zero questions: "Well, you signed up for this study. You have me. Now, what do you want to learn?" For the first week, we had to figure that out and come up with the questions. Once we had discovered that the 5Ws make the best questions on which to organize our inquiry, then they would jump to questioning our questions and the material we were asking about. It didn't take us long to show we had done some basic research so we were asking the right questions about the right stuff. When I got to college, I was really ready because I knew how to approach every course with questions. I thought like

> a researcher, which lead to falling in love with research. Today, I expect the same from all of my students, grads, and undergrads. I think teaching my students to think, to ask the right questions that guide them to collect the right facts, the right data, about the right stuff is my job. (Bellanca, Paul, & Paul, 2013)

At the Denver Green School, upper grade projects are rife with guiding questions. In this example, 6th-graders who were planning a harvest festival came up with their unit's essential question: "Where does my food come from and why should I care?" For each lesson in the unit, they composed specific guiding questions that would provide the needed information: "What are our carbon sources?" "Where do bananas come from?" "What makes a healthy commons?" "What is the ratio between energy and food miles?" "What is in our lunch?"

When students are explicitly prepared to ask productive questions, especially essential questions that can jumpstart inquiry-strong lessons and projects and be extended with guiding questions, there are several benefits as they create a roadmap through their ill defined problem to deeper learning. First, having been empowered to ask their own questions, they are more able to learn the recall information from a course because the memory is based on self-generated need. Second, they have increased their skill with a thinking operation (e.g., "distinguish"). Having mastered the skill, the students are freed to do their own independent inquiries into any course work assigned. Third, they have learned a basic formula for asking their own questions with similar complex thinking verbs wherever "higher order" thinking is called for in the curriculum. Fourth, they are more prepared to use questions that drive the critical and creative thinking processes that advance problem solving (Mayer & Wittrock, 2006). Altogether, these students are no longer dependent on a teacher to feed them each meal; they are ready for their own fishing adventures because they too know how to fish. As is shown in the research on what happens when students learn to fish, teachers quickly see the increased effectiveness of student thinking, the increased achievements that result, and the efficiency by which your students not only cover more ground, but do so much more deeply with deeper confidence (Conley, 2007). Finally, they are more prepared for 21st-century college and careers that are increasingly dependent on the abilities to analyze and understand complex information and solve problems.

SMALL STEPS TO START

Questioning requires multiple opportunities with specific feedback over time. Teachers can start small with activities that are related to specific thinking skills in the standards that lend themselves to development of helpful questions.

Star Model. Pick a key verb from the Common Core ELA Standards. (e.g., *analyze, infer, compare*) to start the quarter. Select a reading task from Standard 10 model texts. Provide students with the definition of the selected key word and a hands-on task for pairs (e.g., *Analyze* the different foods in today's lunch.) Model that analysis task, facilitate the pair work, and discuss how students "analyzed" the food. Move to the literature selection and show them how to do the same analysis by framing a question with the key word related to character, theme, setting, etc. End by asking students to ask an analysis task with some other element of the story or article and assess the examples they create. (Elementary–Secondary)

Invite Engagement. To introduce a new thinking skill, invite students to play a game of pantomime. Teach the rules and start with your example so they can see how to guess with a question that uses a higher order verb. Review the rules and call on different students to enact a favorite literary character, perhaps from a book just read. At the end, generate a list of ideas to post for all to see about which questions worked best and why. Each week, play once and build the list. Invite students to refer to the list for how to find clues with good questions. (Elementary)

Create Cognitive Fluency. Make a bulletin board with a giant concept map (see www.bubbl.us for a template). Read a story (early grades) or assign a short story from Common Core ELA Standard 10. Put the story name at the center and build the 5W questions (who, what, etc.) in rays from the center. Each day, ask pairs to form and share ideas for one of the Ws as a question about the story ("Who was the main character?" "When did . . .," etc.). Brainstorm questions to post for each W and then repeat the daily cycle with answers. (Elementary–Middle)

Invent a Game. Ask student teams to invent a game to challenge other teams in the classroom. Model first (e.g., Team to build the highest tower from paper cups) and provide models of questions they can ask to probe and assess their work. After the game is over, discuss what they learned about solving problems, asking questions, and collaborating. Save the ideas of best questions for all to apply in other situations. (Middle–Secondary)

Assess the Best. Show students a rubric about assessing critical thinking. There are many samples at this site: www.rubrics4teachers.com. Pick a specific skill that fits with a standard appropriate for your class. (e.g., predict, compare, determine). As you proceed through a unit or project, insert 15 minutes per week for peers to review each other's thinking work according to the rubric by asking "To what degree?" (e.g., "To what degree did you make a prediction?") followed by, "Explain why" (e.g., "Explain why you made the prediction here?") (Middle–Secondary)

Make a Research Menu. By turning the word *ASK* into an acronym meaning "*A*ddress the concept," "*S*eek 'why' and 'how,'" and "*K*eep after reasons," students have a mnemonic device for recalling the procedures. Recall is insufficient. Use brainstorming to generate a list of topics interesting to the students. To start each literacy class, post *ASK,* review its letter meanings, and then facilitate an examination of the interest word of the day. (Elementary–Middle)

Question Web. Project a giant web on the smart board. As an advance organizer, brainstorm a list of complex thinking verbs to drive questions about a topic. Post that for all to see. During the lesson take appropriate breaks to allow pairs to form questions they have about a key concept you are studying (e.g. Mobius, Shackleton's Voyage, the Battle of Manassas). Restrict verbs in the questions to the complex thinking operations (e.g., "Why?" "How?" "Predict?" "Evaluate?" "Classify?"Design?"). Discuss why it is important to highlight these verbs. (Middle–Secondary)

Wiki It. Use Fogarty and Pete's "Three-Story Intellect" chart (see Figure 7.1) to build a wiki collection of verbs for asking productive questions. Encourage student pairs to build additional sections applied to differences being studied: "Questions I want to ask about . . . ." (Middle–Secondary)

Be Authentic. Units and projects that drive student motivation begin with authentic questions that are relevant to students' interests. At the start of a required unit, begin by having teams of three generate questions before ranking their ideas from "most relevant" to "couldn't care less." Compile a master class list from each team's top three most relevant questions, making sure that they are asked as higher order questions. (Middle–Secondary)

ReadWriteThink. Go to this NCTE site: www.readwritethink.org, for a collection of grade-appropriate language art interactive tasks. Search the site for "asking questions." You will turn up a variety of interactive tasks to engage students with literacy tasks that promote development of this skill. After an activity, be sure to discuss what they learned about questioning or reflect on how they are improving this skill. (Elementary–Middle)

TAKE GIANT STEPS

Short teachable moment interventions made to introduce students to a skill suffice for making students aware of the opportunity to develop questioning skills. However, to crystallize the skill set, more time and structured work are necessary. The following provides recommendations for crystallizing the asking questions skill set.

A mark that separates teachers in 21st-century classrooms even from those progressive classrooms of past generations is how they emphasize that students learn from the thinking and problem solving they are doing, not just by the doing itself. Dewey's followers in the early 20th century and later followed his admonition to have students learn by doing. This gave birth to the hands-on teaching and learning that survives in the few progressive schools and science classrooms that managed to survive No Child Left Behind. Learning from doing reaffirms the hands-on practices, but adds the proviso that teachers regularly and consistently promote metacognitive reflection so that students look back over what and how they learned or developed a skill. Although this thinking about thinking may present teachers with the most advanced teaching challenges, the value of those teachers' competencies to develop students' ability to reflect on problem-solving proficiency advancement is documented in the reading literature (Efklides & Misailidi, 2010).

Reflective questions about their own thinking separate students' asking of questions related to the content they are studying from their thinking about thinking. Students become their own mediators of thinking and problem solving when an issue prompts that they ask about the quality of their own thinking. In a sense, this is a long extension of Feuerstein's admonition for students to "stop and think." The metacognitive prompts also serve as a practical how-to for teachers who are advancing the 21st-century skill of self-direction or the PISA problem-solving disposition of self-regulation.

Self-regulation of thinking and problem solving begins with prompts that focus on students' targeted cognitive behaviors such as focus, concentration, and precision before proceeding to separating facts from big ideas, making connections, and other cognitive operations.

Simple sentence prompts suffice at the start (e.g., "Today, when focusing, I learned . . . "). Eventually, it helps extend thought when students are asked to give reasons, explain why, provide examples, and compare or contrast with the focus remaining on the thinking skills used for a completed task (e.g., "The reason why I (state specific tactic) to ask questions is . . ." "It helped me to . . . "). In the most advanced form, it is helpful for students to pose and answer questions about their own thinking (e.g., "I wonder what would happen if . . .?" "My guess is that I would . . .").

Once students are showing proficiency at either speaking or writing their responses to their own questions about how they are using a skill, teachers can ask them to apply the thinking to other similar situations or transfer the skill's self-made questions to other content areas or outside school problems.

- "Today, I (skill name) (to do what). What did I do well?"
- "Outside this class (e.g., history), how could I use the skill______ when I . . ."
- "How do I know that I am improving my skill to________?"

To ensure that prompts reflect the student's cognitive growth with questioning, it is beneficial to mix and match oral responses with either a round robin small group response or an all-class round robin with each student completing the prompt in turn. By writing responses to a student-generated questions on index cards, journals (online or offline), and blogs, students and teachers can track positive changes and give feedback on the quality and development of their thinking skills. (Upper Middle–Secondary)

IN SUMMARY

Effects research says that teachers who ask higher order questions raise student achievement. Brain research calls for students to learn how to think and solve problems and transfer the skills involved across the curriculum. Students learning how to ask their own questions is one of the core cognitive skills that enable students to be become deep and highly effective learners. Short interventions prepare students to ask essential questions, probing questions, and reflective questions that enrich the depth of their learning experiences.

Connecting the Dots

- List the three ideas from this chapter that are most meaningful to you.
- Explain why you selected each of these ideas.
- How might you transfer these ideas to your work with 21st-century learners?

He who asks a question is a fool for 5 minutes; he who does not ask a question remains a fool forever.

—Chinese Proverb

CHAPTER 8

Making Connections, Making Sense

It's no wonder that truth is stranger than fiction. Fiction has to make sense.

—Mark Twain

Roger's biology teacher, Mr. Schiller, often told the class the most important things they could learn were "in the textbook." "That's the information you are going to need to finish my science course," Mr. Schiller said. Once when Roger had asked about how photosynthesis worked, Mr. Schiller told him not to worry about that. "Just read. Read the bold text. Those are the important definitions," the teacher asserted. "Just memorize the definition for photosynthesis and you'll pass the test."

Years later after his first tour in Iraq, Roger discovered there was more to learning than memorizing definitions. Yes, he used what he had learned about memorizing when he studied the terrain maps. Now when he prepared his squad, he asked the men and women to tell what signs they had learned to watch out for, what tips they had picked up from other units, and what survival clues they read in the manuals. He always made them explain why a sign was important. He had to break all that data down into parts and examine each precise element. He used every trick he'd learned to make sure the information was accurate and no details were left out. At these times, he was thankful for how his dad had taught him to analyze his work, putting every detail in its place. "You can't make a farm this size pay," Roger remembered his dad teaching him, "unless you check and double check every detail."

In the Army, Roger was putting his dad's advice to good use. Although his dad had taught him everything he needed to know about the cows, the farm machines, and the soil, Roger prized how his dad had taught him to analyze every task that was needed to make the farm operate at a profit. "If you're going to keep this farm, more than anything you need to be a problem solver," his dad had repeated time and again. "Your head is more than an empty milk can."

Later on Roger learned that the thinking he needed in his job was called "convergent" or thinking "inside the box." When thinking inside the box, Roger learned his brain connected the many different bits of information he gathered from reading books and maps, watching, and hearing ideas from his squad. He stored this information and with the new experiences of the moment, he prepared for the next new situation. He took his time to engage what was stored in his brain, examined the many dots, the pieces of information gathered and stored in his short term and long term memories, the remnants of prior learning experiences. With the new experiences to construct new concepts, new understandings, and new insights, he would prepare the squad for its next scouting trip.

Roger discovered that this inside-the-box thinking was called "analysis." He knew that analysis was the skill used to divide an idea, action, or object into is various parts or to make the right conclusion. Doctors, he observed, analyzed illnesses by looking at the many symptoms separately before reassembling the information into a diagnosis. From the many details, doctors match what they observe with prior knowledge so as not to draw a hasty conclusion. He noted that pilots thought a lot like doctors. They analyze the weather conditions and draw conclusions about which altitude may be safest. They look at the clouds, watch wind patterns, check the temperature, store this information, and call it back up the next time they are scheduled to fly. From his high school days, Roger recalled how he had taught himself to think like a scientist. The biologist looks into a microscope, at cell shape, nucleus color, and locomotion of an object before giving it a name. Recalling prior objects from the same group, the scientist draws a conclusion from the many clues provided in the separated parts, the clues that verify if what is observed fits the genus or species the scientist thinks is being studied.

A skillful, analytical mind like Roger's has several attributes. The analytic mind is accurate, precise, and exact in its measurement; it makes detailed comparisons of what is being sensed in the moment with a storehouse of prior knowledge. It reflects on the comparative elements and checks to make sure that it digs beneath the obvious. Above all, the analytic mind looks for the various ways the parts may connect to each other so that the pattern of connectivity becomes the principle focus, knowing full well that there are many clues not visible.

In December, 2009 a man from Nigeria (the "Underwear Bomber") almost exploded a flight from Amsterdam to Detroit with 300 people onboard. After he failed, the public question arose: "What happened? How did this potential bomber get so far through all the security without detection?" After much commentary about which security agency had what prior information, network news channel reporters pounced on the term, "connecting the dots." CNN subtitled its daily report "Connecting the Dots." Almost overnight that metaphor became the cliché of the day, representing the notion that the agencies responsible for preventing such an event had all the information they needed to prevent the man from even boarding the plane in Ghana. They failed to analyze the information, to see the patterns, some obvious and some hidden, that should have signaled: "Keep this man off this plane."

Later investigations into this dot-linking failure suggested that some of the fault lay in too much data flooding the system. Others suggested that all agency analysts didn't have access to all the pertinent data. For those who did, someone failed to make the connections or see the patterns that would have signaled a stop order. A final opinion asserted that the failure was none of these. The failure was a failure of judgment that resulted in an erroneous dismissal of the immediate danger from the potential bomber.

This story illustrates the complexity of making sense in a complex world, especially when that skill must be used in emergency situations with potential dire outcomes. The greater the threat to safety, the more important it is that collected data be accurate, precise, and complete, that the examination be thorough and focused, the judgments sound and logical, and that the hidden connections be verified. The two thinking skills—analyzing and inferring—are central to this process.

THE WORLD OF HIDDEN CONNECTIONS

Among the myriad ways that the analytic mind can make connections of the data discovered, there are four essential patterns that join facts and figures and turn apparently isolated details into meaningful concepts.

The Sequence Connection

When a mind links facts, concepts, or beliefs one after the other in a specific order, the mind is completing the most basic of mental linkages. The order may be set by time, by place, or by importance.

The Time Link. A popular British TV show features a scientist, Dr. Who, who travels through time in a red phone booth. He lands in different time periods. In each time period, he confronts a new challenge. Part of the viewer's challenge is to figure out the connection between the current landing period and others before and after. The more skillfully the viewer pieces together the connections in a sequence with cues and clues from the doctor, the more the program's events make sense.

The Location Link. Individuals who travel away from home learn to distinguish their location by observing details. They fix the unique details and their arrangement in their memory. Once they have seen the rocks of Stonehenge, the white cliffs of Dover, or the pyramids and sphinx, they can easily recall where they are. If they see these wonders in a photo, they can discern where they might like to be. As they travel, one place to another, they arrange their excursion in a sequence.

The Value Link. Vacation prices vary by season, country, manner of travel, hotel arrangements, and other variables. Ads for the same hotel at the same time of the year may look the same or say the cost is the same. To determine real value, would-be vacationers have to look at the fine print and rank the many different possibilities according to "the best deal." Determining that best deal means comparing the value as the individual sees it. By using their own criteria, travelers can put the trips into an order such as most desired to least, least expensive to most expensive, and so on.

The Likeness Connection

Shakespeare wrote a famous love sonnet, "Shall I compare thee to a summer's day?" He then listed the many ways his lover was like the ideal summer day. Sonnet 18 highlights a common type of thinking people do daily: compare or notice how two objects—people, places, events, etc., are alike or the same. In the simplest objects, the task is already complicated. Most objects are more different than alike. When it comes to the more complicated similarities and differences, such as relationships, large institutions and governments, museum quality art from different historic periods, or symphonic compositions by two different composers, comparisons are all the more difficult. To connect the apparently different objects or ideas is a daunting mental challenge that not only involves the senses, but also the analytic ability that differentiates with sharp distinctions as well as bundles the likenesses.

The Cause and Effect Connection

Every time a disaster occurs, scientists work to determine the cause. Part of their challenge is to separate first causes from secondary causes. Yes, there was a tsunami. "What caused it?" is a second level question. The answer is usually "an earthquake at such and such a time and place." The primary question then becomes, "What caused the earthquake?" It is this series of questions that enables them to make cause to effect connections that are reliable and valid.

Other disasters such as auto accidents and plane crashes, lost children, war, and famine are more complex. On the flip side, equally complicated for discovering the cause and effect connection are triumphs that end with an Olympic Gold medal, a warm sunny day, or the discovery of a new medicine.

The Part to Whole Connection

Making a part to whole analysis is very similar to examining two sides of a coin. On the one hand, there are big ideas and complex concepts that bind parts together just as the metal in a coin binds the head to the tail. On the other hand, this type of connection may call for a minute inspection of the details on both sides, an examination of many clues that will lead to the conclusion that the object is a coin. In both cases, rules of logical thinking guide the path that leads to a valid connection.

Big Ideas. Christopher Columbus was a man with a big idea. He dreamed of a great land where he would find abundant gold and other valuables. This idea drove his plan to sail the great sea, find the new continent, and return to Spain with a fortune and its fame. His hypothesis, like the big ideas of other explorers through history—Hudson, Shackleton, Earhart, Fremont, and Glenn—used their dreams to organize their trips and to test their hypotheses about the frontiers they faced. That they might not succeed or might land in a different place than they dreamed as Columbus did, did not take away from their willingness to think big. In a similar way, scientists such as Marie Curie, Alexander Graham Bell, and Galileo challenged established thinking and hypothesized outcomes that they dreamed would make the world a better place. Using the results of many experiments, most of which failed, they put together small pieces of success that eventually proved their hypotheses.

Clues. Arthur Conan Doyle was a pioneer author who popularized best practices by detectives for bringing criminals to justice. He gave his hero, Sherlock Holmes, the skills for taking notice of small clues and combining these clues so that they told a sensible story.

In recent times, TV detective work has shifted to forensic experts who use scientific technology to identify miniscule clues. Some shows use the clues to seek answers to long-cold cases, others take on the criminal investigation in Miami, Los Angeles, Chicago, and New York, making sure that the quality of their work in piecing together the clues arrives at the right conclusion.

Logic. When inventors like McCormick, scientists like Salk, or detectives like Sherlock Holmes complete their work, the logic they used is not often apparent. In some cases, their reasoning was deductive, in other cases, inductive. Logic, therefore, may be considered the glue that holds these two reasoning processes together.

Deductive Reasoning. When Holmes began his investigation of the Hound of the Baskervilles, he started with a hypothesis: "What if," he asked, "the killer was not human?" He then assumed the killer was an animal, perhaps a dog, and proceeded to find proof for his hypothetical assumptions by connecting the tiny bits of evidence: phosphorus stains, a boot, a pack of howling hounds—the clues he found that announced "the killer was a human. The dog was a scapegoat." His deduction came from careful study of the evidence as he tested his hypothesis with the specific evidence. Such is the nature of deductive reasoning, which starts with a law, principle, or hypothesis and is supported with data that verifies the given generalization.

Inductive Reasoning. Holmes didn't form his hypothesis until he had examined the evidence available at the start of his investigations. From the wounds on the bodies, he made inferences that lead to his conclusion about the "wild animal." He used the conclusion to form his hypothesis and then went in search of confirming evidence. Such is the nature of inductive reasoning, which proceeds to form a general statement or conclusion from pieces of evidence.

THE BENEFITS OF MAKING CONNECTIONS

Before children learn to add one and one, they are making connections. Their most important early connections occur when they begin to recognize their parents' faces. Then parents begin to talk with the "show and tell" of familiar toys and sounds. Eventually, they teach with examples. One coin and one coin make two coins. One red car and one black car make two cars. After having counted many different objects, children learn to assume that one and one is always true. From there, they build an entire number system as they learn how to add larger numbers, subtract, multiply, and divide.

The process of connecting number operations makes it easier for children to learn how to count. It also provides a logical certainty that helps young minds make sense of many other connections. When children are able to make many connections using the different patterns or arrangements they establish in their minds to better understand the world outside those minds, that world becomes a safer and saner world to navigate.

MAKING INFERENCES

The more complex the new patterns and arrangements children learn to make, the more it becomes apparent that each child with his or her different experiences forms patterns in different ways. It also becomes apparent that the child needs to find ways to make the recall of those patterns easy, intuitive, and ready for close transfer. Thus is born the need to help the child shift those patterns that are concrete and senseable to those that are abstract and hidden. Later, as soon as the child can connect Mommy's smile with the words "I love you," the smile takes on new and different connotations for that child.

The skill at drawing inferences is dependent on the ability to gather and analyze information. Gathering information is the first phase in the act of learning. When children arrive at school, they start to learn that there are many new ways to gather information from many new sources. In reading, it is not long before students learn how to look at a picture, a restricted set of letters and three spaces to name the object with the given letters in the space (e.g., f-o-x, p-i-g). Lots of inferences are required! Later, learning to gather information and put it together in a pattern helps them understand the character, the place, and the events in a printed story. In science, they graduate to gathering information as they watch balloons float in a tank, observe minute life under a microscope, or piece together fragments in an archaeological dig. With a browser, students research a topic for history class, gathering information that they can organize into a paper or presentation. As they build their own brain-based information storehouses, they bank facts and concepts that they can later connect to make sense of new information from new lessons.

In the second phase of learning, analytic skill plays a powerful role. Analysis operates at two levels: the literal and the inferential. As Sherlock Holmes did after he gathered his facts, students must put aside biases to classify the information gathered and search for recurring patterns. "What detail goes with what other details?" "What combinations are linked in many ways?" "What labels will we use for our new groups?" "What order will we make out of the jumble?" The answers to such questions depend not only on the ability to analyze the literal data collected, but also to draw and use inferences about their meaning.

Because they are no longer in the mode of just gathering new factual information from the world around them as they did in the crib, early grade students must learn to dig into their prior experience, and use their analytic and inferring skills to connect new knowledge with past experience. When they analyze their prior experiences, they not only look at the obvious connections their senses announce are present ("There is *red thick* liquid on this knife."), they must also analyze the red liquid they see ("It is wet, sticky"), pull up the possible connections ("catsup?, blood?, paint?, fingernail polish?") before determining via past experience which is the most likely answer. At this point, they can read between the lines, comparing what they see and smell with other clues present or not present, obvious or hidden, so they can draw conclusions that include a great deal of *inference making.*

Making inferences is more than a literacy skill. When a young mother hears her baby wail, she infers there is a problem in the nursery. Relying on past experience, she must infer the exact reason: thirst, hunger, a dropped toy, or a wet diaper.

Drawing inferences becomes more essential for school, career, and personal success with each passing year. It is school, however, with its emphasis on reading that learning to infer becomes the quintessential thinking skill. While the focus is often on teaching phonics, phonemics, and vocabulary development, learning these basic reading skills are mere stepping stones toward learning to understand the meaning of what is read. Without the ability to infer, students will flounder with weak reading comprehension. With weak reading comprehension, college and career success is compromised.

The inference challenge is most serious when it comes to reading fiction. In plays, novels, and short stories, students are asked to "figure out" a character. The author does not say, "this is a bad man." Instead, she provides clues in what the man says and does and what others say about him. Some clues are obvious, such as when Batman declares that the Joker is a slimy coward. The Joker's words and his interactions with Batman confirm this. Other characters such Hawthorne's Hester Prynne are presented more subtly. Hester wears her Scarlet Letter, a symbol. Inference skills are not needed to know her sin, but they are necessary to understand the many motivations of her heart, grasp Hawthorne's many messages, and confirm the inferences we have drawn with the clues that continue to emerge through the last page of the final chapter. When students finish the story, they do know the events, the site, the location, and the conflict. Not until they join the other clues from her words and actions and the condemnations of those around her can the students infer the full power and meaning of Hawthorne's sad heroine.

Poetry presents an even greater challenge as well as a richer opportunity to sharpen students' ability to infer. Because great poems are dependent on the connotations of the poet's word choice, the analysis of poetry is dependent on the strength of that skill, colored by each person's interpretation of the poem's meaning.

Even in a play, poetry can appear. Shakespeare's plays, for example, can be read as long poems. In *As You Like It,* the character of Jacques did not mean that the globe we live on is a flat wooden stage; he intends that we infer meanings from our personal interpretation of the comparison and what it suggests.The richest meaning is not found in any literal comparison of the words to describe the flow of a play from act to act, but in the figurative interpretations of gloomy Jacques' speech when he compares the scenes in a play to the stages of life. Beyond that, readers can infer what the words mean with their private interpretations derived from prior experience. The greater number of valid interpretations the words provoke, the more universal the literary piece. *The Ages of Man* provokes many different interpretations, each drawing on the individual's life. One high school class produced these individual interpretations:

> We all are different things at different times in our lives: a liar, a hero, a creator, a destroyer.
>
> This is about my granddad. He just died at 92. I knew him in the last stage when he became a little child again, needing lots of care. I find this work very sad, just as I was in his last years.
>
> All of these aspects create us and we often play these roles at the same time. We enter others' lives to accomplish something, good or bad, and then we leave. Our lives also change as we grow and gain wisdom.
>
> To me it sounds like we are the players on God's stage. I mean we all live a life. Here on this earth, and we all have different purposes for being here, and we all come and go.

In informational text, inferring helps students assess whether or not writers are logical and truthful. Do the arguments connect? With the facts given, do we believe the scientific claim? Are we able to judge the degree of bias? Can we analyze the bias? As we listen to the TV newscaster, is she one-sided with her facts? Has the author colored the story with his own interpretation of the facts? How do we know? What inferences help us read between the lines of what the writer is saying?

Knowing how to identify inferences in nonfiction texts, magazines, newspapers, and e-mail blasts enables today's students to listen more carefully for cloudy messages from politicians, news broadcasters, bloggers and Tweeters, and other 21st-century media. "What is fact?," "What is fiction?," "Is President Obama a U.S. citizen?," "Are all Republicans racist?," "Are all immigrants drug dealers?," "My science textbooks say evolution is a fact. Her textbook says evolution is fiction."

The command "analyze" is the most stated in the Common Core ELA standards. From 1st grade to 12th, students are asked to analyze literature and instructional texts across the curriculum in grade-appropriate standards. Although the specific request for students to make inferences appears less often in the *grade level* standards, the skill stands at center stage in the *anchor* standards for college and career readiness alongside analysis.

- Read closely to determine what the text says explicitly and to make logical inferences from it; cite specific textual evidence when writing or speaking to support conclusions drawn from the text.
- Determine central ideas or themes of a text and analyze their development; summarize the key supporting details and ideas.
- Analyze how and why individuals, events, and ideas develop and interact over the course of a text. (Common Core Standards Readiness for College and Careers, p. 1)

SMALL STEPS TO START

It is the little clues in what students read, notice, and hear that provide the impetus for sharpening their skills of analysis. Analysis works best as a skill for breaking the obvious into parts. Inferring contributes by helping students discern what lies hidden below the surface and away from their senses, call upon their prior experience, and ferret out deeper meanings. These activities will advance students' recognition of the relationship between the two thinking skills.

More Than One Way. Select a grade-appropriate poem suggested by ELA Standard 10: Reading Literature. Read it aloud to the class. On the board or smart board, use a word web with the poem's title in the center. Match pairs to agree on what the poem means. Encourage divergence. Record each different response on the web before going back to each pair and asking them to give their reasons for the interpretation. Discuss why there are different interpretations. (Elementary)

Going Shopping. Ask students to invite their parents to make the weekly shopping list together. Ask them to follow these steps:

1. First, brainstorm everything you think you want to buy using a Post-it note for each item.
2. Second, one by one take the notes and put them into alike groups such as vegetables, canned goods, frozen items, etc.
3. Third, label each group. If you have sub-groups in a group, label both the sub-groups and large groups as you complete this part of the task.
4. Go shopping and report to the class how the list helped or didn't. (Elementary)

What's for Dinner? Recipes provide helpful fodder for making analyses. Invite students to bring a favorite family recipe from home or go online and find a favorite recipe for each culture in your classroom. Project it on the smart board or give each student a copy to analyze by underlining all of the needed ingredients with a colored marker. With a different color, invite students to highlight the precise amounts of each ingredient. Make a side list that puts the ingredients into special groups. Label each group. Repeat these steps each time you do a different recipe. Label the process "analysis" and make a definition for the class, identifying where else students use the skill and what steps are important in making an analysis. With this advance organizer, a class is now ready to transfer the analysis procedures to a book analysis as called for in the literacy standards. (Elementary)

Who's on First? Select a short story or novel to read or a favorite drama on TV. Pick one character. After the first third of the story, invite student pairs to describe the character on an index card and tell what clues they used. See if their analysis holds up as they finish the story. Identify what obvious and what hidden clues they missed. (Middle)

What Is the Big Idea? Assign students to read a textbook chapter. Ask students what is the main point the author is making and how they know that. Invite each student to keep a weekly journal in a small notebook responding to the prompt "Chapter __'s big idea is . . ." "I concluded this because . . ." as they provide evidence from the text, noted by page. (Middle–Secondary)

In Conclusion. Give each student pair a copy of an editorial of interest to them. Ask them to summarize what the author said and then write a counter editorial. Share the editorials in groups of four with discussions of inferences made. (Middle)

Who Said What? Provide your class with a list of tasks to analyze for bias:

- Read a magazine article or a *New York Times* nonfiction bestseller.
- Listen to a TV editorial.
- Watch a *Good Morning America* or *The View* panel discussion.
- Listen to a Dr. Phil claim.
- Watch a political debate.
- Watch a Michael Moore movie.

Instruct the students to return with a summary of what they read/heard and an analysis of the presenter's bias (What was the bias statement(s)? What evidence do they have of bias? What inferences does the bias facilitate?). Discuss these questions and determine areas of agreement and disagreement about the inferences made. (Secondary)

Watch Out! When students are listening to someone argue a point (a politician, newscaster, editor, neighbor, car salesperson, real estate developer) there are key words that indicate they may be drawing a false inference. Sometimes, they check to see that the premise is grounded in fact and that indeed, the facts justify the conclusion. Or, test to see if the conclusion is a biased overstatement hiding false inferences. Share these examples to test:

- Since everyone else gets to stay out past midnight . . .
- Seeing that the other Superintendents are paid above $100,000 . . .

- Because the President is a liberal (or conservative) . . .
- The reason is that the Senate has never . . .
- In view of the fact that he/she voted for . . .
- Given the fact that he/she supports . . .
- (Because) Harry's mom lets him . . .

At other times, the signal comes at the end of a statement and indicates, "Here comes a conclusion I have drawn." Again, they must watch out to see if the premise justifies the conclusion:

- So therefore, I should be able to stay out that late.
- It is only natural that we pay ours more.
- Consequently, he will destroy the country.
- Because all its members are _____ .
- It follows that he/she will vote for me.
- I can only conclude that he will bankrupt the country.
- As a result, the end of the world is near.

Armed by these examples, invite students to keep a reporter's notebook. In it, each student is to record at least five statements they hear, use, or read over a week's time. At the end of the week, discuss the students' analysis of this false logic with a focus on false inferences made.

Rubric Brainstorm. With the class, brainstorm criteria for a rubric on drawing inferences. Make this skill central to all reading assignments for the quarter. At the end of each reading task, require students to self-assess how they attended to this skill in their reading. Determine how the final rubric results will count in the quarter grade. (Middle–Secondary)

SEEKING DEEPER MEANING VIA SCAFFOLDS

Students benefit from scaffolded skill development. After learning how to understand a skill, it helps them to move to more and more difficult applications. By targeting the development of a thinking skill such as drawing inferences, teachers can scaffold student applications through careful selections of increasingly more difficult literature.

Cartoon Capers. Go to www.readwritethink.com and find cartoon capers. Assign teams of three to complete a three-to-six panel cartoon on a current event or a made up story the team wants to tell. Distribute markers and large sheets of newsprint so they can hang the results. Invite the other teams to carousel around the room. When they stop at a posted cartoon, they can infer the cartoon's meaning using Post-it notes to declare, "This is about . . . ." When the carousel is done, discuss how they identified the inferences and what inferences were not made. (Elementary)

What Are the Motives? Assign an age-appropriate short story. (See ELA Standard 10 for recommended texts.) Assign a character to each team of three so they can analyze the character's motives. After sharing the results and making sure that there was agreement among groups with the same character, inquire how students (a) analyzed the character and (b) made inferences. Make a class list of good inference strategies and repeat this two-step process in the next two pieces of literature to be studied. Make sure that literature selections increase in difficulty. (Middle)

Explain It. Assign a novel to the class. Assign teams to focus on one element each (e.g., setting, tone, plot, conflict, characters, etc.). Make a giant concept map for all to see. As each team reports on its element, they contribute to the map-making, sure that they can (a) identify the element, (b) explain how it contributes to the theme, (c) note what inferences they had to draw, and (d) what clues they used to draw their inferences. Extend the task so that each student's next reading is a solo choice that follows the same process and ends with an explanation of how the student used the best inference strategies from the team task list. (Secondary)

IN SUMMARY

Making sense occurs when students make connections among what may seem to be disparate facts and figures. This connection making is the coming to understanding at various depths of meaning. The human mind as a pattern maker finds different ways to make sense, including use of logic, cause and effect relationships, likenesses, and part/whole relationships. Through the use of classroom interventions that encourage students to see how connections are best made in different situations, teachers can strengthen students' connection-making capabilities.

Connecting the Dots

- List the three ideas from this chapter that are most meaningful to you.
- Explain why you selected each of these ideas.
- How might you transfer these ideas to your work with 21st-century learners?

I regard the theatre as the greatest of all art forms, the most immediate way in which a human being can share with another the sense of what it is to be a human being.

—Oscar Wilde

CHAPTER 9

Making Judgment Calls

Knowledge comes, but wisdom lingers. It may not be difficult to store up in the mind a vast quantity of facts within a comparatively short time, but the ability to form judgments requires the severe discipline of hard work and the tempering heat of experience and maturity.

—Calvin Coolidge

As children grow up, they learn lessons from their parents and other adults on how to behave, especially when interacting with others. "You gotta be taught" were Rogers and Hammerstein's words in the classic musical *South Pacific.* A key behavior implied by this song is making judgments about other people.

The skill of making sound and reasonable judgments as opposed to biased and judgmental generalizations about individual members of an ethnic, religious, or racial group can be nurtured and developed. This mediation is important when developing young people's skills for making judgments within the many different problematic situations they will face in a lifetime. The act itself calls for students to call into play many of the creative and critical thinking skills they have been improving through their schooling years. Although the situations today's students encounter may be ever changing and made more severe, the need to learn how to judge each situation without bias still remains.

Parents and teachers can encourage children to avoid making far-reaching and biased pronouncements about others based on insufficient information or false and extreme generalizations. In the early years, these parents correct their children when the children announce, "everyone in this family is a loser." They stop their adolescents when the teens scream, "You are the worst parents ever" or proclaim, "He's just another typical (ethnic or racial stereotype)" by encouraging them to stop and think. When parents admonish, "Let's hold on a moment.

Why don't you just stop a minute and consider what you have said?" these parents are taking an essential step in teaching their offspring about tolerance and the need to make judgments based on logical evidence. They reinforce these corrective lessons by showing their children how to make positive *informed* judgments about individuals that identify strengths rather than pounce on weaknesses.

MAKING SOUND JUDGMENTS

Beyond the obvious advantages derived from children and teens making judgments that align with fact when interacting with others who may differ from them, there are many other lessons to be learned about using sound judgment, the act of evaluating or assessing people, places, events, values, beliefs, and actions on documented evidence and according to logical criteria. Here is a partial list:

- On the playground, students encounter bullies. Sometimes, a student is the victim, other times the observer. In either case, students must make judgments about how to react.
- As adults, it is important that citizens make evidence-based judgments when they serve as jurors. Sometimes the cases are simple, such as when predominant evidence showed the guilt of Bernard Madoff. Others, such as the homophobic hate crime at Rutgers University that ended in a suicide, require deep reasoning and close examination of evidence before citizen jurors declare guilt or innocence.
- When students are faced with a college choice, they must dig deeply into the facts about the college. "How does the campus look?" "What is its safety record?" "What majors are offered?" "What is the cost?" "Are there housing alternatives?" "How do graduates fare?" "Who are the other students?" "How good are the teachers?" "Where is it located?" The selection of a college to attend will affect many later choices in a lifetime, not the least of which will be the student's career and the discovery of lifelong friends not yet met.
- The institution of marriage is dependent on each partner making sound judgments about the other's character, dreams,

goals, and interests. During courtship, long-term couples tend to have been those that discussed their mutual likes and dislikes, investigated common feelings, and shared visions of their futures before making the final binding judgment.
- When working for an employer who may turn out to be unethical, individuals must make a judgment about their own integrity. "Do I stay here or go?" "Do I blow the whistle?" "If I stay, do I give up my own values?"
- When hiring for a new position, the law requires that the person who is the decision maker judge on the facts and avoid bias and social stereotypes to reject or to accept an applicant.
- A community faced with an issue that requires consensus (e.g., new street lights, new zoning law, animal control regulations) must dissect arguments, separate fact from opinion, and challenge assumptions in order to arrive at a logical agreement.
- In every election, opinions differ, facts are blurred, and individuals slur their opponents. It is the voters who must check the facts and ensure that their ballots are cast free of bias.

To make a sound judgment, an individual must assess or evaluate the facts that are apparent, separate opinion and bias from fact, and connect the dots of good reasons. Because the process of deciding is complex and involves many thinking skills, the pursuit of precise and accurate data takes patience and persistence.

Without precision and accuracy coloring the logic of decision making, it is easy to fall into the quicksand of judgmental choices, especially when heated emotions are involved. One effective method for working with groups of students slipping into this quicksand is the buddy program based on Roger and David Johnson's well-researched "Constructive Conflict Resolution" (Johnson & Johnson, 2004). This advanced program, grounded in the brother researchers' cooperative learning research, requires students to attend three after-school sessions with a "buddy" from the "other" group. The program's first session shows how words and actions directed at the "other" group can accelerate into hostile confrontations. Snap judgments about the "other" group pushes bad buttons. On other days, students are guided to learn about each other and seek common interests. During different activities they are encouraged to mingle with their new buddies and join in cooperative groups. As students build their social skills, they are expected to show these skills when they are together

In this program, explicit lessons can also help students better understand "friends they did not know." Students can explore the featured skill, "judging without being judgmental." In cooperative groups, students develop a T-chart that allows teams to contrast the skill of "making judgments" with "being judgmental" (see Figure 9.1). The formal sessions end with problem-solving scenarios asking students to apply their newly developed skills.

JUDGMENTS IN ACADEMIC WORK

The cognitive skill of making judgments in the academic side of school is a core skill that is especially important to developing students' inquiry and problem-solving skills. The judgment skill is about helping students evaluate data. What are the facts about the historic and fictional people they are studying? What data are best in a science experiment? When doing research, online or offline, how do students know what information is true? False? Appropriate? Most important?

Each time students read a piece of fictional literature, they must go in search of the text's meaning. Such a search for evidentiary data is the heart and soul of the ELA standard. It is a task that calls for one judgment after another: "What do I think this word means?" "How does the context change the meaning?" "How do all the words together tell me the meaning of the story?" "How does this quotation from the text show that I have made a sound judgment?" "What other text do I quote to support my case?" "Does that text evidence come from what the author says?" "From what the author has a reliable character say?" "What evidence do I have from the text that the character is reliable?"

The analysis of informational text is somewhat easier than fictional text. Informational text in magazines, news articles, Facebook status updates and blogs usually deal with what is said. It is literal. There is seldom intention by the writer to suggest multiple meanings. But then, there is the challenge of who the author may be and what his or her biases might be.

In informational text, a reader must determine what judgments have to be made to ensure that even what appears to be literal informa-

FIGURE 9.1. T-Chart

Making Judgments	Being Judgmental
facts	jump to conclusions
look before you leap	dirty looks
words	half truths
proof	rumor
get evidence	no idea
reasons	no proof
be sure	lies and insults
exact data	feelings
accurate	wild accusations
understand	half truths
talk	gut feelings
check it out	glares

tion is truthful, backed by facts. It is more difficult for readers to analyze literary text. In this text, the author may add a cloud to disguise a character's meanings. Nuance, irony, metaphor, and other devices raise the level of difficulty when it comes time to judge not only the person, but his or her words, the words of others, and the author's intent.

More than any other cognitive function, students must rely on their judgment-making skills to sharpen precision and accuracy in gathering facts, selecting data, making sense so as to extract meaning and solve problems. In addition, making judgments is a complex skill that blends a variety of other thinking skills into the evaluation process. This includes the evaluation of inquiry lessons or problem-based learning projects that intentionally ask students to investigate data. For instance, students who are starting an inquiry project about the Inca Empire have a digital problem to solve as soon as they browse the assigned topic on the Internet. Immediately, the browser tells them that there are 1,300,000 available online sources. Relying on what they know about making systematic searches (see Chapter 3), the students preview the first page of available sites: Wikipedia, IMAGES, National Geographic Pictures, Inca for Kids, Nova: the Lost Inca Empire, Inca Explorers. This leaves 1,299,994 citations to go. Which to choose?

A scan of Wikipedia (with all its known weaknesses) provides an outlined overview of the topic and presents ideas that will allow students quickly to narrow their search. However, Wikipedia has a reliability problem. Immediately, students must call on their judgment-making skills. How do they decide what to select from this easy to use, but less than reliable source?

REFINING AN ONLINE SELECTION

Selection of the exact topic they want will depend on the students' readiness to evaluate the online options. Three procedures can guide the judgments they will make as they evaluate sources.

Adopt a set of standards with criteria. Students may know something about standards: what they are and why they are important. For instance, there are quality standards for manufacturing automobiles, planes, and boats. These standards give assurance that the vehicle is safe and in sound operating condition. Food standards communicate that the purveyors follow the rules in preparing edible food. School standards set the bar for a high quality education. Medical standards tell the buyer that the maker is concerned that the medicine produced will not have side effects.

Identify the criteria. Criteria are a more specific set of benchmarks or signposts that tell the students that they are on the right track in their search. With benchmarks they can create a measurement scale so they can contrast what it is they are measuring (e.g., "A is more important than B"). Important signposts should designate that the author has relied on credible sources, has a credible reputation, is knowledgeable in the field, and is publishing with a credible publisher in the field.

Apply the criteria. Each criterion measures each idea, topic, or object being considered. Essentially, students are asking, "Which topic is more suitable to our interests and the assignment?" Their answer should respond to the question, "To what degree does this action satisfy my search?" (e.g., "To what degree does the author quote published sources in respected journals or newspapers?")

FIGURE 9.2. Narrowing the Topic: A Sample Rubric

This topic ___________________________

1. is very interesting to us. (3 points)
   Yes Somewhat No
2. fits the overall assignment. (3 points)
   Yes Somewhat No
3. will help us to frame an essential question. (3 points)
   Yes Somewhat No
4. will lead to expert information. (3 points)
   Yes Somewhat No
5. will introduce us to other resources. (3 points)
   Yes Somewhat No
6. fits our ability to do a good job. (3 points)
   Yes Somewhat No

Total Score: (High:15–18; Medium: 12–14)

Before students initiate a data search, such as one about the Inca Empire, a scientific principle, or an author's point of view, it will help to check their prior knowledge about this three-step evaluation process itself. Teachers can do this by checking keyword vocabulary knowledge (e.g., *criteria, benchmark, scale*) or by asking students to make a sample rubric that includes these three procedures. Teachers can help by inserting an explicit lesson that shows students how to create a rubric or provide the students with a rubric about making judgments (see Figure 9.2). With this, they can provide students with the common vocabulary that will guide their judgments.

After reading and comparing sub-topics, groups can select the top scoring item before moving on to find information that might enrich their inquiries. This process allows each group in a classroom to select a unique topic under the same master topic heading. For the Inca search, the topics selected might include sub-topics such as Machu Picchu, the Sapa Inca, The Kingdom of Cuzco, The Spanish-Inca Conflict, or others. The self-selection process allows for groups to differentiate the topics according to their own feelings of competence and interest.

To ensure that the judgment-making process is not lost in the content nor blocks students' development of their judgment-making skills in future projects, it is beneficial for teachers to review the students' command of the judgment-making process. "What did you learn about setting your own standards?" "Criteria?" "Benchmarks?" "How do you think you can apply what you learned in other projects?" "Other classes?" "Outside class?"

INFUSING JUDGMENT-MAKING SKILLS INTO THE CURRICULUM

There are two basic questions for teachers to ask about infusing the judgment-making skill into curriculum. The first question asks about students who have no experience with the skill: "How are they started?" The second question asks about transfer: "How are students best enabled to apply the skill in and outside the curriculum?"

For the first question, teachers can start with the essential question: "What are the strategies that work best to introduce students to the skills inherent in making sound judgments about text?" The basic response is explicit instruction. Explicit instruction allows teachers to isolate the thinking skills they are targeting and build a series of strategic lessons that will promote the skill's fullest development.

When using explicit instruction about a thinking skill such as "making sound judgments," experience-rich inquiry lessons are an especially effective strategy (Marzano Research Lab, 2012). Inquiry lessons contain multiple research-supported strategies that include an advance organizer, an essential question, three question-driven phases, student reflections, and formative assessments (Bellanca, 2010). A sample explicit inquiry lesson for the middle grades is shown in Figure 9.3.

When teachers guide students through the inquiry approach, they can evaluate their lesson design with the six guidelines from the Institute for Educational Statistics. After selecting the specific Common Core State Standard grade-appropriate text to use with the inquiry strategy (Standard 10), they talk *with* students through a model lesson. A teacher's questions illuminate the key elements in the thinking process for making sound judgments from the point of view of a character. For instance, using the short story, "The Most Dangerous Game," the teacher asks about the victim's judgments and how these impacted his

FIGURE 9.3. Topic: Making Sound Judgments

Advance Organizer: Read the story "Three Little Pigs." Ask "Which of the pigs made the best decisions when building his house?" "Why?" Solicit several different ideas.

Essential Question: "How do I make good choices that keep me safe?"

Phase 1: Strategy: Read Frost's "The Road Not Taken" (Standard 10, Grade 6, CCSS-ELA). Have pairs respond to the questions: "What are the choices the rider was asked to take? What choices he did make and what were the effects of each?" On the Smart Board build a class matrix with non-duplicated responses.

Phase 2: Strategy: Invite each pair to go online and find a definition of the word "judgment." "What does it mean?" Using that definition, they are to evaluate (judge) the decisions of the rider. "How good or bad were the decisions?" Select three pairs at random to share their answers or post the answers of all pairs on a blog (http://www.kidblog.org). After reviewing these responses, discuss what it means to "make a sound judgment."

Phase 3: Strategy: Ask the pairs to answer the questions "What does making a good judgment mean to me?" "What are some times in my life when I used good judgment?" "What was the result?" After they develop answers, show three webs on the board and call for unduplicated responses. Conclude by asking students to make a general rule from the responses.

Student Reflection: Ask each student to make a journal or blog entry. "It is important for me to make good judgments by ______________ because ______________."

Assessment: Ask each pair to complete a pre-made rubric that assesses their judgment by these criteria: took our time to think, took our time to consider alternatives, looked for reasons, and gathered evidence.

escape. In this ask-through, teachers also inquire about the strategies and tactics the victim is using to make judgments. That first phase is followed by phase two, guided practice, during which the teacher sets up a series of questions for student trios to ask as they guide them through the next piece of literature. Teachers provide formative feedback as the students make their first application of the mental menu with more challenging text such as a novel or play. When it appears students are making comfortable applications, the teachers move students to the third phase, independent practice, where the students apply their judgment-making skills with the study of more challenging texts differentiated by each student's readiness (Bellanca, Fogarty, & Pete, 2012).

The reading materials, the questions, the vocabulary, and tasks for children of different ages and reading readiness will differ in each of the seven inquiry strategies. If there is not age-appropriate literature given in Standard 10, teachers may substitute a favorite reading level-appropriate poem or short story that involves multiple decisions about making judgments (e.g., "Humpty Dumpty," "The Masque of Red Death," etc.). To continue to an advanced focus on this thinking skill, teachers transfer students' skills into studying a more difficult play or novel (e.g. *Harry Potter, Raisin in the Sun, Macbeth,* etc.).

SMALL STEPS TO START

A second option for teachers to introduce or advance development of this critical thinking skill includes intentional and engaging interventions that promote students' reflection on their development of the skill, provide advance organizers, or provide products that enrich students' problem solving. At appropriate times, teachers decide when to interject these activities into the daily schedule. For instance, if they need an explicit lesson on a sub-topic such as making judgments about people or places, "write a poem" is an appropriate phase three activity. If they need students to practice a sub-skill such as clarifying information, teachers can insert PACTs (see strategy description below) into an explicit lesson that includes guided practice of skills for clarifying information about a conflict situation.

Write a Poem. Invite students to write acrostic poems (see http://readwritethink.org) that reflect their knowledge of being nice to other people. Hold a discussion about what it takes to be nice to others, accepting their faults, etc. Help the students reflect on how it felt to have someone be nice to them. On the smart board, build a list of ideas before showing them how to write the poem. (Elementary)

Make a Storybook. Invite students to draw a picture of a person doing something to help another person. After sharing and discussing pictures with a partner, students draw a second picture to show what might happen next. Stopping and sharing the words that go with each event, each makes a book cover and back with title, subtitle, and other typical cover features (see http://www.readwritethink.org). They post the books and discuss with the class the ideas in their stories about being nice to others. (Elementary)

Stop and Think. Make practice of the judgment skill into a quarter-long project for upper-grade students. When students meet someone new or enter a new situation, pause, gather the evidence, and weigh the details. By stopping and reflecting, rather than jumping to a conclusion without weighing all the facts in the situation, students can stay more objective and weed out biases. At the first opportunity after the encounter, the students reflect in their journal about how they suspended judgmental thinking. (Secondary)

Probe. When students face a challenging situation, they can learn how to probe those involved with open-ended questions. "What do you think . . ." is a strong starter. Other strong starters are "How do you think . . ." and "Why do you say . . ." expressed in a sincere tone. These questions allow the person with whom they are interacting the choice to respond as they wish and give as much information as will help make a judgment. Single answer questions (e.g., what?, who?, when?, and yes or no?) make it tougher to get all the information you may need to make a judgment. Set up pairs to develop the probing skills. After they read a short story, one person takes the role of reporter. The second is a main character from the play. The reporter uses probing questions about why the character made certain choices. The pair reverses roles after the first interview. When done, the pairs discuss and then share with the class their findings. (Middle–Secondary)

Use PACT. As a follow-up to probing questions, students can adopt PACT (Paraphrase statements, Ask for alternatives, ask to Clarify, and Test options). The reporter, perhaps in CNN style, mixes and matches these questions to help identify *all* the information needed to understand the interviewee and his or her motives for the responses:

- *Paraphrase:* "If I have caught the gist of what you are saying, I think you said . . ."
- *Ask for Alternatives:* "What other ways to you think we might do this?"
- *Clarify:* "Can you give me some examples of how else you think this happened?"

- *Test Options:* "Let's think of some other tactics that we could try." (Middle–Secondary)

Chart the Facts. When faced with judging a character in a story, it helps students to use visual charts. Start with the *newspaper chart*. It will prepare students to dig out all the facts in the situation before jumping to a conclusion. Head five columns with the questions "who," "what," "when," "where," and "how." Using a story recommended by the grade-appropriate ELA Standard 10, help student teams gather all the evidence needed to judge a character. After they have recorded the basic facts, make a sixth column, "why," and interview other students about the character. Tell them to keep those answers that seem most reliable because the "why" responses match up best with the other facts. Accept no "why" that is not backed up with evidence. If they are unsure of some of the "why" responses, instruct them to complete a *plus/minus chart* in which the students list the pluses, the minuses, and the intriguing questions about the completed newspaper chart. (Middle–Secondary)

Junior "What Ifs?" After reading a story to elementary students, ask them to analyze the main character telling why they think the character made the big choices in the story. Ask them to use the text to provide evidence based on what other characters said or the main character said. Ask the class to come up with what these choices say about the character and then pose several "what ifs" for them to discuss. "What would have happened if he had done (a) instead of (b)?" Conclude by having students rewrite the story from the second point of view and set their text into an accordion book (see http://readwritethink.org). (Elementary–Middle)

Senior "What Ifs?" When students are in a situation that calls for making an informed judgment about what is the most sensible thing to do, common sense says to consider the worst possible scenario as well as the best possible outcome. Instruct students to divide a sheet of paper in half then think alone or with a friend about what might be the worst possible outcome if they had decided to do what they were being asked to do. Put this into an historic situation (Lincoln and the slave issue, Washington at Valley Forge, or other historic moments captured with a document such as found in ELA Standard 10). In the selected case, they can consider the worst catastrophes before making a list of the great things this would do, balance one column against the other, and then make a decision which could be "Yes," "No," or "Maybe" with these conditions. Invite sharing among the class and debate the different responses. End with a ranking judgment of the responses discussed. (Middle–Secondary)

The Other Point of View. Pair students for a role play as an advance organizer for a lesson on point of view. Ask them to step into the shoes of another person who holds a point of view that is different from theirs about a conflict they are having. They role play the conflicts and identify the facts and opinions of the other. After examining why the person might hold that point of view, they discuss what changes must be made to arrive at an agreement. (Elementary–Middle)

Bumper Stickers. After students have completed a "making judgments" TV show in which they have analyzed how different characters made judgments that affected the outcome of the story, invite teams of three to create bumper stickers with an appropriate statement that captures what the students learned about decision making. (Middle)

Summarize and Compare Points of View. When friends or experts are giving students different points of view and all responses seem valid, it helps that they sit down away from distractions and write a summary of each point of view. In the summary, they start with the main idea that one person is making. Encourage them to be as true to that person's point of view as they can. Repeat this with the next point of view. It may help to then put each view in a Venn diagram to chart visually the sameness and the differences, considering all the entries carefully before they make a judgment (see Figure 9.4).

To start students learning this process, select a short story, novel, or play that allows for discussion of point of view. Use the process so they can play the role of a character, summarize that character's point of view, and then engage in a discussion with other characters and their point of view. After looking at a character through the character's eyes, ask the students to identify what they have learned about "walking in another's shoes." (Middle–Secondary)

Seek Expert Opinions. Through our age's ready access to information via technology, it is easier for current generations to seek expert opinions prior to making judgments. Some TV shows even allow us to

FIGURE 9.4. Venn Diagram

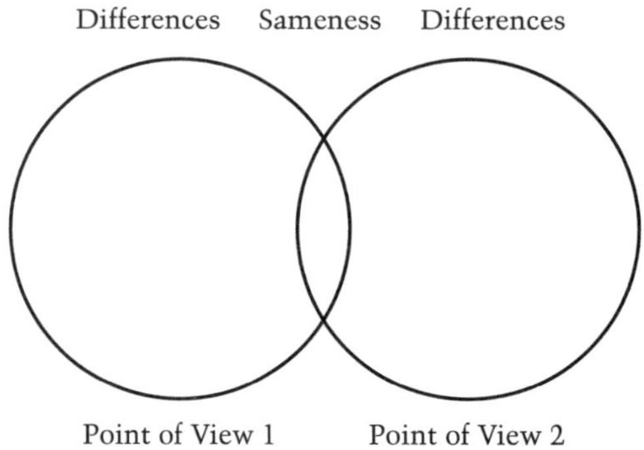

appear before a judge to have the decision rendered by an expert. To find expert opinion, students browse the Internet for a term or question. This act will provide them with a list of websites that will overload them with expert opinions. They need to be adept and unbiased in the selection of the expert. How do they do this? First, they look at the experts' credentials. Second, they look that the experts are free from a biased point of view (a political party, a religious or group affiliation, an explicit bias statement, connections to other online entries which are limited to a single group or point of view, symbols, etc.) Third, they read the material to find how logically it makes its argument, the evidence that it supplies, and the documentation. They can also check out how well the expert is esteemed by other experts, even when they disagree.

Having found the experts, students can make a chart (e.g., the newspaper chart) to gather information and arguments from the expert. If the experts are all in agreement, fine. If not, students must compare the points of view and weigh what each has to say. (Secondary)

REAL WORLD SCENARIOS

Real world scenarios provide students with motivation to develop the skills of making sound judgments while they read, write, and speak in mock trials. At each grade, the teacher selects the literary genres or stories, which experience says are the books most popular with students in past years. In this way the teacher is predicting their continued attraction.

Lego Law. Preview three books for students to review. Give a brief sales pitch for each before inviting students to decide on which story they want to read (this can be individual choice or an all class vote) After they finish their story, working in teams of three, students will decide on what type of house the main character would live in. With Legos, they build the house. All the houses are placed on a table. In turn, each team explains why they built this house with its special features. The teacher is the contest judge and gives different surprise awards. End by discussing with the students how the picks were made and explain the idea of criteria for making judgments. Conclude by asking each team to record its criteria for its choice. (Elementary-Intermediate)

Defending the Genre. Select three literature or information texts to "sell to the class." Invite each student to select one. Set the reading time. At breaks in the schedule, teams of three to five with the same book begin to prepare a list of reasons to defend the choice made in common.

When the due date is reached, all teams meet to finalize their lists and prepare to appear before a jury of peers with the teacher as judge. Each team is charged with defending the continuation of the book/genre (both/either/or) on the teacher's recommended list. When one group is presenting, 12 rotated students are randomly selected to serve as the jury. The presenting team has 5 minutes to present its case and will respond to questions from the jury and judge for up to 5 minutes. The jury then votes. A majority "yes" is needed to continue. The judge may select any juror at random to explain his or her vote. To close, the class will discuss the judging process including how they made their criteria. (Intermediate-Middle)

Community Experts. With the class, identify a loose, locally authentic social problem to solve. Divide the class into teams of three to five. Each team will work through the problem to its recommended solution. Each team will argue for its solution before a panel of community experts such as the city librarian. The presentation must include a visual aid other than a collage. The panel will render its verdict and explain its judgment. Each team will prepare a final summary of what it learned about preparing arguments and being judged. (Middle-Secondary)

IN SUMMARY

Along with the information tsunami that increased the volumes of information available on any topic, the challenge of making judgment calls increases in difficulty with each decade. So does the complexity of the task. Relying on other critical thinking skills and cognitive functions explicitly developed in the curriculum, students can learn how to inform their judgment by learning how to develop criteria and applying them in real world, authentic situations.

Conneeting the Dots

- List the three ideas from this chapter that are most meaningful to you.
- Explain why you selected each of these ideas.
- How might you transfer these ideas to your work with 21st-century learners?

Experience does not err. Only your judgments err by expecting from her what is not in her power.

—Leonardo da Vinci

CHAPTER 10

There's Always a Better Way

When you innovate, you've got to be prepared for everyone telling you you're nuts.

—Larry Ellison

When Ford was tired of the horse and buggy, he was alleged to have noted, "There has to be a better way." He removed the horse and added the crank engine, put rubber on the tires, and found a way to steer the horseless carriage. Look at what car showroom visitors have for today's choices:air conditioning, 40+ miles to a gallon, Bluetooth and GPS, backup mirrors to check following drivers, speed controls, hands-free parking, and not far in the future, cars that will drive themselves. And still, today's auto designers follow Ford's alleged dictum, "Just find the better way."

A defining characteristic of Americans is their entrepreneurship—the endless drive to improve whatever they want—from soup to nuts. Americans are never satisfied. America even has been labeled "the innovation nation" (Kao, 2007) as its citizens look for a better way in what and how they eat, sleep, work, and enjoy themselves. Sometimes they make changes to an already favored object. Some make the pizza thinner, thicker, larger, or ready to go into a deep dish. Others add to the object. On the pizza, they put tomato, cheese, and mushrooms, all the leftover veggies in the refrigerator and even pineapple and yogurt.

If additions are not enough, others find ways to make the object smaller or rounder or squarer; they cut holes in it or, like the horse and carriage, make it run faster, smoother, and with less gas . . . or no gas at all. Sometimes, as with the stove, they make new combinations by adding an oven, a microwave, or an alarm. The boundaries are limitless, even with extra big risk takers jumping in a space suit from 23 miles above the earth just to see what benefits *might* result.

In the 21st century, the innovation drive has expanded beyond American shores. Like the motion picture, the cotton gin, the automobile, and the many other fruits of its creative minds, America has exported its inventiveness as well. The drive to modify something old to make something new or to transform a common, old item, requires little more than a sharp mind that thinks outside the box and takes risks to act in a novel or different way. More and more, it matters less and less where that mind lays down to sleep . . . Italy, Abu Dhabi , Singapore, or New Delhi.

Most can recall the names of successful inventors who made a major impact on their lives—Da Vinci, Deere, McCormick, Edison, Gates, Salk, and Walton. More likely, most can name little items that have made an even bigger impact on everyday lives without knowing the inventor's name. Who invented Liquid Paper, the paperclip, the web cam, or microwave? What about the Wiki, Thinsulate, blister packs, or the trailer hitch?

What successful inventors show us, whether the result is a better pizza, a touch screen, a rose bush that has no fungus, a car that can fly, or an HPV vaccine to prevent cancer, is that thinking outside the box for any improvement can pay handsome rewards. Better yet, it shows that taking the time to look for a better way when individuals or a social group are not completely happy with what they have is a worthwhile risk, one that can enrich their quality of life as well as the lives of millions whom they will never meet.

LEARNING TO THINK OUTSIDE THE BOX

In essence, *divergent thinking,* also called *creative thinking,* the thinking that occurs when the mind stretches beyond what exists in reality to consider new possibilities, is as important to problem solving as critical thinking. Is it possible that like its partner, convergent or critical thinking, creative thinking can be taught? How possible is it for one student to become a divergent thinker comfortable with having a single train of thought that leads inextricably to one answer to a problem or one way to do a task, step by step in a set order? Can schooling expand students' risk taking and develop their willingness to examine alternatives and generate other courses of action? If so, how beneficial would it be to have students who are as strong divergent thinkers as they are convergent thinkers? Would it increase their achievement? Improve their mathematical problem solving? Strengthen their ability to problem solve across the curriculum? Prepare them for more rigorous application of mind skills in a biotech curriculum or to address issues of financial literacy? Could 21st-century society absorb hundreds of thousands minds bent on changes, improvements, substitutions, replacements, and transformations?

The 2012 PISA frameworks suggested not only that the answer is "yes" to each of these questions, but that the "yes" is an imperative. Like critical thinking, creative thinking has "gotta be taught" (*South Pacific*), a belief reinforced by thinking skill guru Edward de Bono (1999), who wrote "Intelligence is something we are born with. Thinking is a skill that must be learned."

In 2012, the PISA assessments included two frameworks; one to assess mathematical problem solving and one to evaluate cross-curricular problem-solving abilities. The obvious goal is to measure how well 15-year-old students from 30 or more competitive nations can perform the types of mental tasks that their global economic systems demand. Because it has become a 21st-century data truism that assessment drives instruction, it is a safe bet to assert that problem-solving acumen will receive increased instructional attention from those schools whose nations are battling for economic superiority.

Inherent in the PISA 2012 leading-edge problem-solving assessments was the search for students' ability to think divergently. The PISA test makers have assumed that critical and creative thinking skills are integral to the nonlinear problem-solving process. This makes clear that the PISA frameworks for 2012 are adding another nail to the coffin of those educators who are holding fast to old instructional methods and a curriculum model that itself needs a substantive, transformational reconstruction. Although the trickledown effect may take some time, it is very likely that in this decade American teachers, principals, and even the architects of their schools will be pressured to increase the amount of innovation they generate far beyond what they do today.

In the first decades of the 21st century, school reformers, yet shackled by the No Child Left Behind construct, limited innovation to tweaks—minor modifications of the school plant (paint the walls, add computer labs); the curriculum (increase time allotted to basic skills, buy test prep materials); instruction (scripted, direct instruction remediated with costly tutors and mentors, drill and practice with costly technology, reward high attendance with money and prizes); assessment (increase number of test days for formative and summative exams, test prep booklets); and leadership (comply to Annual Yearly Progress, or AYP, evaluate teachers on student performance, review data weekly, turnaround schools by changing staff). Little risk was required for these or other much hailed and punitive quick fixes such as uniforms and more stringent behavior codes with infraction fines. Small risks indeed do produce small gains.

At best, evidence that these minor adjustments have impacted rigor or results, has been slim (Zimmer et al., 2009;) if at all. Even if minimum mutations to the classic educational assembly line model did increase student achievement and make more students as college ready as some claim, few adaptations have done anything to make the deep alterations that the world outside of schools is demanding so that more students stay in college and earn degrees (Harvard Graduate School of Education, 2011). That task has been left with others who understand that such minor modifications, whether in traditional public schools or in charter schools, are not the final word for changes required in 21st-century schooling.

CHANGE FROM THE OUTSIDE

Yes, there are teachers, schools, and districts that are trying to break the No Child Left Behind mold by defying the pressures that say, "keep inside the box." On a scale of zero to ten, the preponderance of change in these first decades has kept the scale tilted to the zero end with improvements being more a throwback to the 1950s than coming from innovative thinking about what the future will demand.

To move across the change continuum to see deep and significant innovations that challenge a poorly productive status quo or look to the future on how to save a life rather than a single limb, is indeed difficult. School change has never been easy.

Those who want to make the changes needed for this century have never been faced with such staggering odds, especially considering how political and educational leaders seem determined to add additional testing days that reduce instructional time within the school year, uniforms, scripted instruction, and test prep tutoring sessions as the tools that will bring improved results. Add to this the multimillions of educational dollars wasted on the testing industry that shortchanges the professional development that provides the greatest chance for teachers to raise student achievement and develop 21st-century skills with proven innovations such as project and problem based learning infused with technology.

In spite of the wasted funds dedicated to the superficial refinements of obsolete school change efforts, there are efforts that are making substantive changes in the American schools. In New York City, IBM, the MacArthur Foundation, and City Colleges have joined together to establish outside the box schools. Here are a few examples:

- The School for One uses technology to schedule students in individualized programs with daily computer adjusted schedules.
- The Quest School is a product-based-learning middle school driven by game theory. Its faculty are experimenting with innovative ways to advance students' curriculum via the games that students design.
- P-Tech is a fast track to college admissions. Working with a science- and technology-heavy curriculum, the faculty is preparing students for college careers in entry and midlevel jobs in high tech companies after earning early admission to a City College program. Chicago hopes to replicate this model with five schools sponsored by high tech companies including Cisco, Intel, IBM, Verizon, and Microsoft.
- High Tech High in Southern California was started as a public charter school in San Diego. High Tech High is now a network of 11 K–12 charter schools and a university with campuses throughout San Diego County. High Tech High was originally conceived by 40 civic and high tech industry leaders in San Diego, assembled by the Economic Development Corporation and the Business Roundtable. This group met regularly from 1996–1998 to discuss the challenge of finding qualified individuals for the high tech work force.

  The schools are designed to serve the needs of a diverse, lottery-selected student body in an "its work that matters" environment that reshapes what classrooms look like. Teachers are prepared at the High Tech University to guide peer collaboration in a work-centered, standards-aligned curriculum that relies on technology and product-based learning as the primary mode of instruction. With 35% of its students as first in the family to go to college, 100% of its students are admitted to college with 30% preparing for STEM careers. The High Tech Foundation secures the philanthropic support to operate the schools. The record of High Tech High, available on its website (www.hightechhigh.org) speaks strongly for the success of its outside-the-box approach. With 100% of its graduates accepted at college (80% at 4-year schools), its high school sits among the top performing schools in the state.

- New Tech Schools are noncharter and charter public high and middle schools in 70 districts from California to New York state. Most are in small urban districts or rural districts. Like High Tech High, technology and project-based learning drive the standards-based curriculum. Designed as small schools (with maximum student bodies of 400), New Tech High Schools highlight project-based learning, 1:1 computing, integrated courses, school culture, and deeper learning. Most start-up New Tech Schools are supported by local industry such as Cummins Engine (Columbus, Indiana) and Samsung (Manor, Texas). Like the more recent P-Tech in New York, New Techs send high percentages of their graduates to college. Many of these schools become leaders on their state's standardized tests in spite of starting with low-performing student populations.

TRANSFORMATIONAL SCHOOLS

Statistics from Manor New Tech High School, in a rural community near Austin, Texas, contribute to the case supporting innovative transformation reform models over the incidental implementation and replication of the assembly line models that did so well in the 20th century. The new models not only top the achievement charts, they show students with increasingly strong 21st-century skills. Unlike the heavily subsidized turnaround schools, which are enamored with efficient and obsolete assembly line instruction and are showing zero to minimal improvements, the new tech-style schools rely on project-based learning and technology to enrich student learning and produce significant results.

The results created after the reconstruction of a well-worn middle school in rural Manor, Texas, demonstrate what can happen in a small school that makes deep changes that would have been unrecognizable to most of today's parents.

Manor New Tech High houses 400 students. Unlike schools that make themselves "small" but continue to rely on skill and drill instruction and other superficial throwbacks to the 1950s, this school and almost 120 others across the country transform what is most important: the quality of instruction. Since traditional squared classrooms were replaced with double-size classrooms observable through a wall of hallway windows, Manor's students now study in a variety of workspaces using their own iPads or one of the iMac and PC workstations that line two walls. In a 74-minute period, some students work in small groups, some alone, and some in teacher-led workshops. Whatever the academic discipline or integrated courses, project-based learning supported by technology dominates instruction.

In the 4 years since teacher teams initiated co-design of projects aligned with the Texas Standards, the state assessment results have climbed in a hockey stick pattern. In 2012, Manor New Tech was near the top among all Texas high schools as its students' scores belied the demographics expectations. Math and science scores carried students into the top percentile while language arts/social studies topped the charts at 99% (see Figures 10.1 and 10.2). Fifty percent of Manor's graduates are the first in the family to graduate. Many are sought out by prestigious universities from across the country. More impressively, district leaders, some who had lead a fight against the New Tech alternative, have changed their minds about the value of transformational innovation as represented in the New Tech deep learning approach. In 2012, responding to the 4-year uptick of standardized test scores, Manor New Tech initiated a professional learning academy, Think Forward PBL Institute, for incoming new faculty. The success of the Institute reinforced Manor's school board initiative of transforming the District to project-based instruction, infusing 21st-century skills into learning, and integrating technology into daily teaching and learning. Within the next 5 years, it is anticipated that all district schools will have adapted the approach.

As promising and powerful as these innovative results sound—major leaps in student performance, new family representations in college, STEM-ready graduates, students with well-developed 21st-

FIGURE 10.1. Manor New Tech Performance Data, Math and Science Results

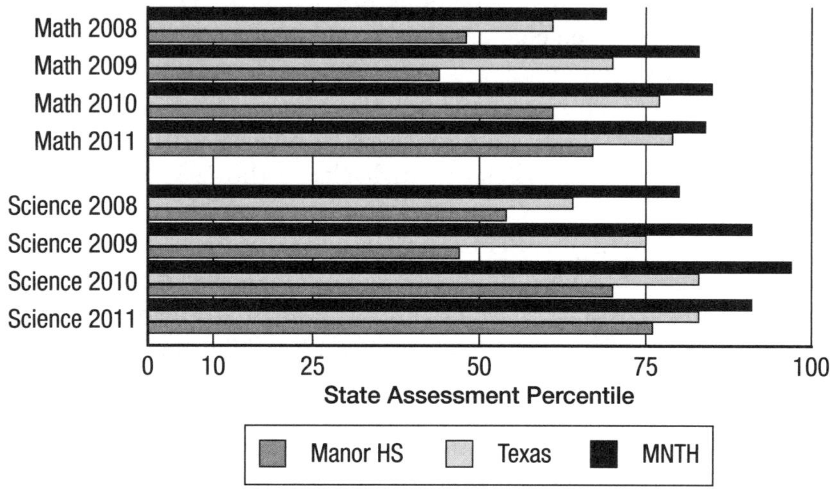

Source: Manor New Tech, 2011

FIGURE 10.2. Manor New Tech Performance Data: Social Studies and Language Arts Results

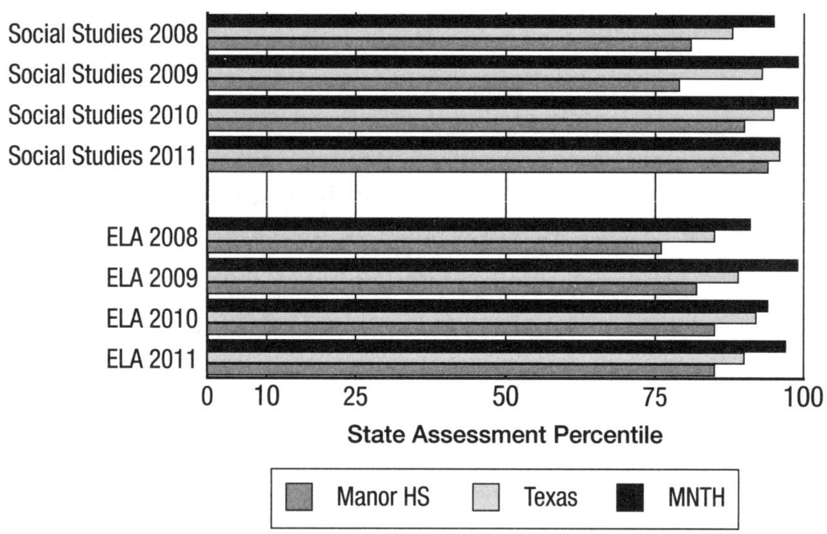

Source: Manor New Tech, 2011

century skills and ready for increased problem-solving challenges in 21st-century careers—the relatively small percentage of innovative schools still leaves the innovation scale heavily tilted to the zero sum side.

Even when other promising and innovative schools such as the Expeditionary Learning Consortium, the Expedia Schools, or the Project Schools, or schools in a countable handful of districts that are adopting P21's Mile Guide or its 21st Century Tool Kit, or schools that are awarded prizes by high tech companies for adopting one-to-one technology or adding STEM initiatives, the numbers of schools that are willing to risk serious innovative thinking and modification so that all students are immersed fully in 21st-century instruction is miniscule.

If the movement toward whole school reform continues and becomes a trend, the number of innovative teachers is likely to follow the upward movement of test scores found in schools such as Denver Green Expeditionary School, Stockton Elementary School in Chicago, Holly Elementary (Michigan), New Tech, The Rock Island Mathematics and Science Academy (Illinois), and others who provide the proof that big risks do bring big gains not just in achievement test results, but more important, in the skills students garner to succeed in a global work world. Not only will communities see teachers thinking creatively, they will see their children following suit.

SMALL STEPS TO START

To jumpstart the return of innovative, divergent thinking to the classroom, teachers can enter the fray by degrees. First, they can integrate the proven tools of brainstorming, webbing, and concept mapping as tools to expand students' right brain fluidity and flexibility as well as to enrich students' understanding of reading materials and their solving of mathematics and other cross-curricular problems.

Second, they can blend the creative thinking engendered by these practical tools into daily problem-solving tasks. The tools are especially helpful with problem solving in nonmathematical curricula. Students can discover how to expand their innovative thinking by developing talent with the digital versions of these creative thinking tools.

There are three basic tools that initiate and then expand divergent thinking. All are built on the thinking skill of generating multiple responses (i.e., facts, concepts, ideas, values etc.) at key spots throughout the problem-solving process (e.g., problem examples, synonyms, attributes, strategies, solutions).The most basic tool, brainstorming, is a strategy for thinking that enables students to construct many variations of a desired result. As such, it enables students to make more skillful use of the idea web, the concept map, and other graphic organizers that generate multiple responses. Each of these tools is adaptable in multiple ways in lessons and throughout the problem-solving process.

The Brainstorming Tool. The brainstorming tool is the basic outside-the-box thinking tool. It develops the divergent thinking skills that pair with analysis and evaluation throughout the problem-solving process. It stretches student patterns of thinking by helping them explore options prior to making the best selection. It also provides a valuable tool for developing their disposition for flexible and fluent thinking. Flexible and fluent thinking are two attributes key in innovative thinkers' disposition repertoire. They are essential for those individuals who must examine ideas from multiple perspectives, seek novel ways to adjust the commonplace, and find new solutions unique to new problems.

Sharpening the brainstorming tool allows students to hone key skills. As they become more fluent and flexible, students learn when and how it is best to suspend judgment, keeping every possible idea on their "worth considering" list. In the classroom, collaboration sets the climate that enriches development of the divergent skills, skills for which Edward de Bono filled a tool kit of activities and tasks. By turning to such easy-to-adopt tools as think-pair-share or cooperative trios (Bellanca, 2010), teachers can establish a culture of respect for divergent thinking and facilitate a host of daily activities that not only enrich the brainstorming tool with ways to enlarge, make complex, simplify, adjust, add to or subtract from an idea, but also to ensure that students have explored sufficient possibilities before making a crucial decision in the problem-solving process. (All grades)

The Idea Web. This is the most basic visual brainstorming graphic organizer. Many teachers have relied on the web to help students recall the many ideas they may have gathered from an experiment or informational text or to identify the attributes of story characters the students will compare in a discussion. These are all valuable applications of the organizer. Other valuable uses range from using the tool to show the whole class science or social questions generated by pairs in a think-pair-share or show ideas for making an essential project question or for selecting the product a team will make at the end of a project-based learning unit.

In the context of problem solving, teachers want students to use webs to generate their own ideas as well as sharpen the ways that they do so. At the first level, teachers can have students count the number of ideas they list on a web. At a second level, teachers can ask students to group and label the generated ideas. At the third level, they can ask students to evaluate the ideas or the groups with criteria the class generates. With these criteria, teachers can encourage students to evaluate their divergent thinking not only for number of ideas, but for quality. At the fourth level, teachers can target phases of the process for improving idea generation by working students to the point where they are brainstorming criteria and evaluating each phase with these same criteria prior to narrowing the selection (i.e., ideas for an essential question, ideas for guiding questions, ideas for assessing data sources, ideas for evaluating products). (All grades)

Generating Quantity. On a sheet of paper, invite groups of five to draw a circle and radiate from it 12 to 20 lines outward. In the center, the recorder will enter a word or phrase from a current unit of study or topic of interest. Invite students to look at the word from a single point of view such as its good characteristics: Cabo San Lucas is sunny, warm, fun, full of options, a great fishing town, etc.; Its drawbacks: Cabo is crowded, expensive, hard to get to, noisy, etc. Invite the teams to see how many descriptors they can generate. If a team reaches 24, push it to 36, and so forth. Select different interest topics that the class is studying: A character from a book, a science conundrum, a class rule, a new web 2.0 tool. (All Grades)

The Concept Map. The concept map is a complex word web. It encourages students to generate ideas and then to connect these ideas with visual lines that represent different types of connections. Strong concept maps rely on students' ability to generate ideas as a first step.

The more adept students are at generating ideas, the richer the concept map. Like webs, concept maps are a proven method for gathering information from text and preserving the connections. They are equally as valuable as a planning tool. In this mode, the maps, also called "mind maps" assist students in looking for better ways to accomplish a task, expand an idea or invent a solution.

Invite student teams to draw a concept map from a projected sample. Invite the students to start with a single high interest concept and branch out to as many first round concepts as they can generate. For instance, start with a new math concept such as fractions. Enter the concept in the starting circle. Brainstorm ideas associated in branched circles. From each branched circle, brainstorm other words. Continue the branching as far as the edge of the paper or use an online map. Finally, connect ideas among the branched circles with colored pencils.

Use this to (a) gather prior knowledge, (b) summarize a lesson, and (c) build ideas throughout a project. At the end, review how the tool helped with idea generation and how both helped with understanding the concept. (Middle–Secondary)

VARIATIONS ON A THEME

One idea leads to another. The same is true of the different classroom activities and strategies that can develop students' idea generation skills as they look for the better ways to solve problems.

The Early Morning Wakeup Call. Start the class period with a team brainstorm. Greet the class with an open-ended question on the smart board: "How many ways can you think that . . . ?" Pose a mini-problem relevant to the class or current events (e.g., history: "How many ways could Allied leaders have stopped Hitler sooner?"; current events: "How many ways can you improve your college application?"; literature: "How many new ways could you get friends to do your chores?" (a la Tom Sawyer)). Teams brainstorm until class roll is complete. Sample five ideas from the teams and then proceed to the day's lesson. (All Grades)

More and More. End the last period on Friday with a brainstorm on ways to improve brainstorming. Start with pairs, combine lists in groups of four, and then in groups of eight. Make an unduplicated list of ideas, post it, and use it as a guide for other brainstorming activities during the month. (Middle–Secondary)

Energizer Bunny. Divergent thinking energizes sleepy or bored students. After lunch or later in the afternoon, take 5 minutes to brainstorm ways to improve thinking about the task they are doing: solving word problems, generating ideas for a project, looking for to make a task easier, etc. Have each student pick from the final list and enter it as a goal in his or her journal. (Middle)

Exercising Outside the Box. Developing students' divergent thinking is often a question of giving a lot of practice and building a disposition. Regular exercise with divergent thinking is as valuable as regular exercise for the body. To ensure that there is variation, teachers can brainstorm or build concept maps about "best times to brainstorm." Reading Edward de Bono's many books will give fodder for brainstorming activities and add a plethora of good ideas that develop problem-solving skills or deepen understanding about core content. (Middle)

Puzzle Pieces. Go to a toy store. Find the puzzle section and find several hand puzzles that challenge students to unravel them. The Rubik's Cube is an example. Have students spend 10 minutes a day unraveling a puzzle and explaining how they generated ideas in order to succeed. Once students have solved a puzzle, try it backward, again looking for a better way. (Elementary–Middle)

Brainteaser Practice. Browse "brainteaser" on the Internet. There students will find a number of sites that provide free brainteasers to play with. Many make fun tools that promote thinking in a different way. (Elementary–Middle)

Super Heroes on a Wiki. Set up a wiki for your classroom. Start with the brainstorming of a list of superheroes your students know. Randomly assign one hero to each group of five students. Instruct each group to create a super villain to oppose their superhero. Show them how to use a concept map to brainstorm all the possible changes. They then draw a picture of the two conflicting characters and prepare to explain how/what changes they brainstormed. Make a list of the best tactics for a poster for future reference. (Middle–Secondary)

Our Dr. Who. Invite the class to watch *Dr. Who.* Discuss his travels to different times and places. Brainstorm a list of places and times your students want to visit. Then ask teams of three to design their own time travel machine out of a familiar object (remember, Dr. Who travels in a red phone booth). (Intermediate-Middle)

No Right Answers Allowed. One of the most effective ways for students to come up with better solutions to old problems is to break the habit of looking for the one "right" answer or the answer they think teachers want. Students can learn to look for *many* possible answers. When they think of multiple solutions, they will generate more and more ideas that build on each other and lead to better ideas. Invite them to remember that Thomas Edison ended his personal invention convention by setting quotas for his new ideas. He looked to make a minor invention every 10 days and a major one every 6 months. He ended up with 1,092 patents.

The next strategies each call for a different approach that will make thinking outside the box helpful to solving problems. They are more complete activities than the easy-to-use mind stretchers above. Each pushes students to acquire a new mindset that results in a new product or a new way of solving a problem and keeps their minds from being stuck in the mud. Each will help students change their pattern of thinking from convergent and analytical to divergent and creative. From the experience, students can reflect on how thinking can purposefully change a mind to look at every problem in different ways. (Middle)

That Is a Good Idea. When a group collaborates on an innovative project, they increase their odds of improving a project tenfold. Ideas get piled on ideas. This cooperative strategy is an effective tool for improving an object or event. It starts with any standard item that the group wants to make over—a lamp, a knife, a chair, an extension cord—or with a more complex item such as a kitchen stove, a pickup truck, or an air conditioning unit. There is a set procedure that follows these steps to extend the group's divergent and outlandish ideas with

FIGURE 10.3. That's a Good Idea

Idea	Reason
1.	
2.	
3.	
Etc.	

a lot of good humor and support for thinking differently. (Middle–Secondary)

1. Identify the object to improve: ___________________
2. One person starts by saying: "A way I would improve this _______ would be to (add, subtract, modify, etc.) _________________."
3. The next person to the starter's right must respond. "That is a good idea because ___________________." Having given a positive reason, the person earns a turn to say: "And I would improve it by _________________________."
4. The next person to the right repeats: "That is a good idea because____________" and adds the next improvement.

Each person in the group takes a turn for at least two cycles. As the ideas are presented a recorder documents the improvements and the reasons on a chart that all can see (see Figure 10.3).

5. When the cycles are finished, the group works together to draw the new object with all the improvements. Everyone has a marker to contribute to the final rendition which is then named by agreement of the members.
6. When the group finishes the drawing, members can go round robin once again and tell how the process enabled them to think differently and how they might use a similar tactic to improve an object that they use every day but that just doesn't seem to do the full job they want. (Intermediate-Secondary)

IN SUMMARY

Divergent thinking is the twin sibling of convergent thinking. With convergent thinking, the mind is looking to analyze ideas and see the relationships of part to whole. It operates inside a logical framework that has precisely honed limits, rules, and procedures. It is inside the box. On the other hand, divergent thinking is meant to take the mind outside the limits of the frame. It is outside the box. In problem solving, divergent thinking is best practiced by generating ideas and differences and sub-differences. Quantity is the first goal. Quality, marked by the grouping of similar ideas generated, is the second, but equally important goal. New studies are showing that problem solving is less about following a set of procedures and more about how the thinker applies both divergent and convergent thinking to the right procedures in the right ways.

Connecting the Dots

- List the three ideas from this chapter that are most meaningful to you.
- Explain why you selected each of these ideas.
- How might you transfer these ideas to your work with 21st-century learners?

If you strike upon a thought that baffles you, break off from that entanglement and try another, so shall your wits be fresh to start again.

—Aristophanes

CHAPTER 11

Mediating Problem Solving for Deeper Learning

Deeper learning delivers the skills and knowledge students will need to succeed in a world that is changing at an unprecedented pace.

—The Hewlett Foundation

Robert Hutchins is often quoted as having said, "It is not so important to be serious as it is to be serious about the important things." When students have the opportunity to study the important things in the classroom, their curriculum is getting close to the rigor that drives their minds to deeper learning in whatever subjects they study. Even when students' study includes mastery of basic skills such as grammar or sentence structure, the *application* of this foundational information benefits their deeper learning when the outcomes are intentionally transferred to "the important things."

21st-century rigor begins with the chance for students to identify issues and concerns they feel are serious and important. In this global, multicultural, and high tech economy, teachers will have a major responsibility for assisting students to meet the challenge of increased rigor. For this it is imperative that they raise their game, just as athletes must raise theirs when they enter world class competition.

Seldom will teachers or students find relevant content discussed in the textbooks they lug around in their backpacks. More often than not, these books, fattened with facts and eye-candy graphics, were outdated before their print dates. This is especially true in the sciences, both physical and social. In addition, these and texts from literature, mathematics, and other disciplines will do little to prepare students with any significant skills for serious insights into the learning tools that lead to deeper learning.

If students' omnipresent and expensive textbooks don't advance rigor, how do teachers assist students, especially those who have been lulled into a passive learning stupor as accumulators of endless teacher talk? The answer lies in a paradigm shift regarding teachers' primary role. In the 21st century, the teachers' dominant role needs to be as the mediator of learning experience. One of the first times this role appears on the learning stage is when teachers use questions and feedback that prompt students to think about the big ideas that make learning important and significant.

Since the middle of the 20th century, prominent students of learning including Guilford (1971), Sternberg (1998, 1999), Sternberg & Grigorenko (2007), and Feuerstein, Feuerstein, and Falik (2010) have provided insights into the relationship of domain-specific knowledge and cognitive processing systems that make for rigor in learning. From these psychologists' insights, it is clear that rigor is found most in the balance of significant and authentic course content with intentional development of cognitive skills. The more students are challenged to transfer content that they value as relevant and important into new and different situations across the curriculum and outside of school, the more accurate it is to describe a course of study as rigorous.

DRIVING RIGOR IN THE CLASSROOM

In the 21st century, the working definition of rigor is far more complex than definitions formed in prior eras. The 21st-century definition suggests that rigor in any course of study is derived from a dual requirement that ends only when a learner is able to *apply* highly functioning cognitive processing skills to mastery of content-specific knowledge. This transfer is true in both the "near" sense within a single area of content as well as in the "far" sense into other disciplines or in work outside the school walls.

Teachers can drive learning transfer at two levels. The first level requires only minimal adjustments in how they instruct. At this basic level, teachers can adjust direct instruction so that they add transfer tasks prior to guided practice and extend practice so that students make applications to high interest or authentic topics. In addition, teachers need only to move the practice tasks farther from their workbooks and worksheets into activities that require students to use their higher reasoning skills within the more authentic topics.

First Level Rigor. Consider this example from an ELA writing curriculum. In the obsolete treatment of grammar from prior eras, teachers were asked to explain and demonstrate a rule such as the correct use of the question mark before checking for understanding. They then turned students to Warriner's grammar text with its hundreds of pages of practice samples. Students "practiced" the rule by identifying which samples showed correct, *near* application of the rule, and which samples were not correct. After practice, students checked their answers as right or wrong, closed Warriner, put their answer sheets in the desks and moved on to the next isolated study. In the next week, they would repeat the same process with a different end mark such as the exclamation point. Today's students might practice checking those answers on a computer with, one hopes, the teacher taking time to discuss the right and the wrong to illuminate the rule.

In the 21st-century deeper learning paradigm, the teacher's role changes in this basic level. A teacher may well introduce the grammar rule and then provide students with opportunity to apply (application is not practice) the rule to 20 to 30 samples that lack any punctuation marks and check for their understanding. In addition, a teacher may move the application bar a bit further away from the rule by asking students to practice the rule by writing their own examples before they explain how they followed the rule.

When does deeper understanding arrive at this basic level? Deeper understanding will begin when teachers move from the *close* or *near* guided practice in which students apply the grammar rule in workbook samples. These book or sheet samples may or may not make any real sense to the students, other than their recalling that all sentences need a specific punctuation mark.

At this point in the basic level, it is time for teachers to put away the worksheets, whether the format is digital or paper, and call on students' thinking skills. First comes the opportunity for students to generate ideas for topics from their own interests and concerns. Second comes the chance for students to work in teams to generate ideas for questions about those concerns, perhaps by webbing questions (see Chapter 4) or by creating a newspaper matrix with questions to ask(see Chapter 9). Third, students, alone or in teams, write their questions and punctuate them according to the rule. Finally, students share their sentences and explain how and why they punctuated each.

By embedding the punctuation task in topics generated by students from their interests, teachers move the transfer bar toward the *far* end of the transfer spectrum, which will make the deepest impact on their learning. After bundling all the end punctuation rules amassed during close application, teachers can embed punctuation practice in other activities, which include writing tasks such as summaries and reflections. Primary students can create sentence stems in which they are asked to prepare sentences with three different punctuation marks. Middle grade students can write summaries that start with a rhetorical question and include at least one example of each mark correctly used. Secondary students can graduate to a five-paragraph essay. In all cases, the language arts teacher prefaces the assignment with a review of the rule(s), reasons, and the expectation that students purposefully concentrate on correct usage.

Transfer for deeper learning of grammar or other basic skills doesn't end in the ELA classroom. Elementary teachers can continue reinforcement of the rule with intentional transfer to writing assignments in other content areas. As they do so, it is important that they remember to prep a high student interest task with expectations for correct usage and take time for students to reflect on what they have done to apply the rule in this other-discipline task. This conscious movement to tasks that connect critical and creative thinking with the content, as plebian as students might judge it, helps teachers mediate the deeper learning of that content.

Second Level Rigor. In the second level, the intentional integration of critical and creative thinking skills within problem-solving scenarios with meaningful content becomes the touchstone for the most serious rigor. The intentional development of problem-solving competencies thus becomes a required condition for determining academic rigor in its most salient aspects.

PISA's 2012 definition of the problem-solving construct establishes a high international bar: "Problem Solving is an individual's capacity to engage in cognitive processing to understand and resolve problem situations where a method of solution is not immediately obvious" (PISA, 2011).

PISA's 2012 problem-solving framework not only describes the critical and creative thinking skills that make up the competency in mathematical and cross-cultural problem solving (e.g., formulating problems, reasoning, connecting concepts, and judging solutions), it asks that students do so in real-world scenarios that they will face in daily living. This new standard calls for students to gather together and apply a battery of critical and creative thinking skills as well as "attitudes, motivation and values" that dispose them to react as problem solvers across the curriculum and outside the classroom walls (PISA, 2003, 2012).

This cross-cultural example illuminates the second level definition. It involves both mathematics literacy and financial literacy. An 8th-grade class faces the challenge of planning a school menu. Parents and students have expressed dissatisfaction with cost, nutritional value, cultural selection, and variation. The problem, stated as a goal that will end with a novel solution that aligns with their state's science and health standards, is strongly felt, and very loosely structured with well-defined problem components. The teacher allots 6 weeks for the problem-solving unit with two central outcomes geared to apply mathematics to financial literacy. The mathematics component will require students to learn how to estimate and apply that cognitive competency twice: to the cost of debt that the students will have to pay on money borrowed in the short term for their project, and to space allocation for serving tables and other equipment. In addition, the teacher intends to build in a wide range of cognitive tasks that will challenge students to compare and contrast, synthesize, interpret, and extrapolate from financial information.

After showing students how to make estimates with algebraic formulas aligned with the standards, the teacher will move them to the problem-solving activities that stress the reasoning processes of modeling and persistence (CCSS, Introduction to Mathematics, p. 5). After completing computer simulations for near transfer, the plan builds in expectation for the far transfer as the students use their mathematics to calculate their interest expense and to lay out the new dining space. In addition, the teacher allots time for student teams to reflect on the mathematical reasoning processes that ended with the students' budget and the architectural rendering.

BEYOND SKILLS: THE PROBLEM-SOLVING DISPOSITIONS

What does a disposition (the amalgamation of values, motives, interests, cognitive processes, and mindset) have to do with problem solving? A literary examination of the term illuminates its value in a 21st-century classroom.

Shakespeare's Hamlet declared he possessed an "antic disposition" reinforced by his tendency to play the role of the "melancholy Dane."

He wandered about Castle Elsinore while brooding on his father's death, his mother's infidelity, Ophelia's confused love, and every other relationship he had.

Hamlet was like a flower with a tendency to grow toward the light. Ironically, he grew toward the dark. His perpetual sadness moved his inclination to the dark side, favoring gloominess over delight. This was the quality that identified him with a frame of mind that defined the state of his soul. It was the sum of his physical appearance, including his black clothes, his emotions, and his way of thinking which lead to his rejection of Ophelia with murder, blood, and sword fights as his predominant problem-solving tools. Even his paean to Yorick, the dead jester, adds detail to the painting of his dark mindset.

The word *disposition's* synonyms—*temperament, inclination to act, character,* and *nature*—refer to the combination of traits which explain the essential and dominant tendency for a person to act in a consistent manner. Choices made spring from the person's disposition to resolve problems in a consistent way by bringing to bear how he or she processes information in mind and heart.

History is replete with figures who exercised a strong problem-solving disposition. Faced with a challenge, their inclination was to solve the problem with optimism and confidence (think of Hannibal facing the Alps), patience, and persistence (think of Confucius creating his law canon), risk taking (think of the Trojan Horse), capped with sheer, unadulterated bravery (think of Amelia Earhart). When mixed together with finely honed thinking skills, these dispositions resulted in unique personalities driven to overcome any and all situations by turning on the problem-solving switch that drove their personalities

Ordinary citizens with the problem-solving disposition stand out from those who tend to sit and watch. Their stories pop up on the nightly news. For optimism, browse Nick Scott; for patience and persistence, browse Liz McCartney; for unadulterated bravery, remember Rosa Parks, the Tuskegee Airmen, or the firefighters at the Twin Towers. With that special attitude of mind that favors alternative solutions over giving in, giving up, or being overwhelmed, these men and women faced their challenges and overcame difficult obstacles one after the other. Theirs was truly the "willingness to engage with such situations in order to achieve one's potential as a constructive and reflective citizen" (PISA, 2011).

In order for American students to become disposed problem solvers, more will be required than memorizing procedures that contribute to problem solving. First, there are the skills or competencies necessary for producing artful and novel solutions (Mayer & Wittrock, 2006). The skills, however, are insufficient if they can't be applied. The ultimate challenge, the biggest problem as seen from the disposition perspective, springs from the need for a nation to turn out high school graduates with strong dispositions as effective problem solvers who possess "cognitive skills required to solve unfamiliar problems encountered in life and lying outside traditional curricular domains" (PISA, 2011).

Getting Ready. In the 21st century, a more difficult test faces American students than those challenges that faced past generations. This will focus on competencies that require deeper understanding of domain-specific knowledge as well as high level interactive problem-solving skills. In the 2012 problem-solving framework, students may have seen problems such as these:

- Caught in traffic congestion, how will you use a GPS to navigate the fastest route to the nearest hospital?
- With a seriously ill family member, you must use a new mobile phone that lacks specific call directions. How will you summon aide with the phone?
- At the airport, you are assigned an unfamiliar ticket vending machine. You are running late and don't understand how to access this machine. How do you get a ticket in time to get through the long lines and board?

Solving an interactive, open-ended problem is only part of the test. Because the given problem will hide relevant, needed information, test takers will have to make and test inferences. To do this, they will be asked to explore alternatives, represent the problem, develop and test hypotheses, and make plans. How well they perform these operations will be important in judging their level of competence.

A Preview of a Coming Attraction. If the PISA 2012 Framework for Problem Solving has its anticipated impact on America's standardized testing program, the U.S. Department of Education funded Partnership for Assessment of Readiness for College and Careers Consortium (PARCC) and Smarter Balanced Assessment Consortium (SBAC) will develop Common Core Standards-aligned national tests that are balanced and challenging. With balanced assessments, these tests will examine students' proficiency in applying the national standards to real world, authentic, simple, and complex problems. The consortia have indicated that they intend to give priority to the examination of rigorous content, but not to the exclusion of performance tests that will test students' ability to perform *application* of knowledge tasks.

If American schools are to ready students for such tests and meet the CCSS goals to ready all students for college and careers in the 21st century, there are significant instructional implications. First, in mathematics, the CCSS Introduction announces that its first priority is preparing students to make sense of problems and persevere in solving them. In the early grade standards "mathematically proficient students (are those who) start by explaining to themselves the meaning of a problem and looking for entry points to its solution. They analyze givens, constraints, relationships, and goals. They make conjectures about the form and meaning of the solution and plan a solution pathway rather than simply jumping into a solution 'attempt.'" In the upper grades, "Mathematically proficient students check their answers to problems using a different method, and they continually ask themselves, 'Does this make sense?'" (CCSS, Introduction to Mathematics, p. 5).

This Introduction continues with detailed descriptions of seven additional proficiency groups that overview the higher expectations for thinking and problem solving about the mathematics content. These state that the standards will guide students to reason abstractly and quantitatively, contract viable arguments and critique reasoning of others, model with mathematics, use application tools strategically, attend to precision, look for and make mathematical structures, and look for repeated reasoning by others (CCSS, Introduction to Mathematics, p.1). A final paragraph calls for students to "connect standards for math practice to standards for math content" as they show how well they understand and use mathematics in the early grades to how they solve, prove, represent, explain why, and evaluate mathematics. These often repeated verbs suggest that any balanced examination of student content must include examination of the complex thinking proficiencies that guide students to proficient problem solving.

One implication of these new standards falls on classroom teachers. For those who have relied predominantly on procedural recall to teach mathematics, the framers of the new standards did not throw the baby out with the bathwater. They recognized the value of procedural knowledge. However, they also emphasized that such knowledge is only a small part of what students must learn to do as mathematical problem solvers, the ultimate goal of the Common Core Standards' makers. Instead of putting problem solving as the last step in the mathematics curriculum with the least amount of allotted time or incidental treatment, the framers placed problem solving at the top of the list where it becomes the top priority, starting in kindergarten. Every mathematics class from the first day of kindergarten through grade 12 is asked to begin instruction framed in the problem mode so that knowledge can proceed to its application. For those classrooms that lack a teacher ready for this shift, schools will have to provide adequate professional learning and time allotments to enable the change.

PISA's "Framework for Problem Solving" pushes the envelope one step beyond Common Core's expectations for mathematical problem solving. The 2012 document calls for problem-solving competencies to inform the entire academic and nonacademic school curriculum with "cross curricular problem solving." It does so because these competencies provide a window for observing students' competencies for transferring basic thinking and other general cognitive skills via the far transfer challenges outside school walls (Lesh & Zawojewski, 2007). Theirs is a cross-curricular thrust stressing that the competency list must include solving open or ill-defined, messy problems of increasing complexity, abstraction, and levels of difficulty across all domains. In the 2012 PISA exam, technology-assisted testing will allow for examining how well students are able to achieve this higher call for complex thinking.

The Time Is Now. For "yes but" responders to this push for problem solving and deeper learning, multiple examples exist that are preparing students to be successful world-class problem solvers. Teachers in schools such as Manor New Tech High School and its 70+ siblings across the nation, the High Tech High Schools, the Envision Schools, the Expeditionary Learning Schools, and the Project Learning Schools are already implementing instruction that marries content and thinking skills. The Quest Schools in New York and Chicago are experimenting with game-based projects while Chicago's Stockton School, Glen-Ellyn, and Mannheim, Illinois schools have joined schools in Michigan, Alaska, North Carolina, and Oregon to saturate students' daily learning experiences with project-based learning units that develop problem solving proficiencies as well as address the standards. In addition, selected secondary teachers at schools, prepared for problem-based learning by the Illinois Math and Science Academy, focus on the problem-solving process with student-generated and authentic issues.

Various school districts such as Newport News, Virginia; Auburn City, Alabama; Catalina Foothills, Arizona; Manor, Texas; Columbus, Indiana; New York City and Albany, Middleton Wisconsin, Indiana; and Napa Valley, California are turning greater attention to project-based learning or the Partnership for 21st Century Skills' thinking skill laden curriculum (P21, 2012). With these schools in the forefront, other districts, schools, and individual, self-directed teachers scattered at random districts across the country are starting to follow suit. Not only do students learn the thinking skills and make close transfer to academic problems of high interest, they are given the chance to investigate problems of high interest that encourage far transfer.

Pushing the Envelope. With minimal adaptations, teachers comfortable with direct instruction can initiate their own shift to high transfer instruction that leads to deeper learning. Their challenge is to extend the application of standards-aligned skills with intentional transfer through their curriculum. For this, it will help when they create learning tasks that hold high interest for students and promote the critical and creative thinking skills needed for transfer. For making significant improvements that lead students deep into what they are learning, teachers will turn fuller attention to organizing instruction in problem-solving units that lead to the deepest learning and most far removed transfer possibilities. Teacher professional learning programs such as the Illinois Consortium's MindQuest21, Buck Institute of Education, and the New Tech School Consortium provide in-depth project-based learning preparation guided by Project-Based Learning (PBL) experienced practitioners.

ON YOUR OWN STARTERS

For teachers making their own move to a more problem-driven approach that aims from the start at deeper learning, tactics that focus on students learning about how to problem solve have great value. Remembering to add the various questioning and giving feedback focused on students' thinking and problem solving, the following strategies will be helpful starters.

Seeing Is Believing. Go online to www.ilc21.org and click on "Resources" and then "Free Video Downloads." On the home page and other pages throughout this site you will find other vetted PBL school and district samples of videos from PBS and the schools themselves. At the site www.iriinc.us you will find video that shows demonstrations of mediation in the classroom. (All Grades)

Make A Visit. If possible, go visit one of the schools that is practicing PBL and critical thinking. Call ahead for an appointment. For assistance, contact the Illinois Consortium via e-mail at: info@ilc21.org. (All grades)

Jump in. In mathematical problem solving, students are introduced to problem solving by the Common Core State Standards with concrete problems in the first grade: The first standard in this section asks students to solve word problems that call for addition of three whole numbers whose sum is less than or equal to 20 (e.g., by using objects, drawings, and equations with a symbol for the unknown number to represent the problem) (CCSS.Math.Content.1.OA.A.1).

Each year after, this same statement is presented, but in a more complex form. Don't sit around and wait the district to say "Go." Here is a starter tactic that can be adjusted by grade level.

- Start by providing student teams of three with a box of 20 crayons and paper. Ask each team to group the numbers so the sum of the groups is equal to 20. Have them replicate this arrangement following the formula of x = ___+ ___+___.
- Students may use either numbers or objects to fill in these blanks. Discuss the various strategies they use to solve the problem.
- Record the strategies on a list for the bulletin board.
- Each week, present a new problem to solve after reviewing the listed strategies. (Elementary-Mathematical)

New Endings for Old Stories. Read a story to the students. Select a story with a set number of characters (three pigs, seven dwarfs, etc.). Invite pairs to find another way to solve the characters' problem by telling what the problem was, what different choices the characters had, the new choice, and why it was selected. Ask the pairs to represent the new story in a book format. Post the book and discuss the thinking the students did to come up with different endings. Record their ideas for generating different endings and review them each week with a new transfer task. (For a book pattern, go to www.readwrite-think.org). (Elementary, Cross-Curricular)

Open It Up. Ask open-ended questions to mediate student thinking about their problem solving. Highlight the four processes that will be central to PISA exams (PISA 2012, 55-58): (1) "What were some different ideas *explored* by your team?"; (2) "How did you *represent* your ideas in the book?"; (3) "How did you *plan* the book?"; and (4) "What did you *learn from* retelling a story in a different way?" Set up a wiki that allows all to contribute and build the answers for each questions over multiple experiences. Hold classroom discussion about how these questions guide problem solving. (Elementary-Middle)

Process Poster. Select a middle grade geometry standard (CCSS Mathematics Content, 5.G.A.2). From the text, select three problems of increasing difficulty that match the standard. Begin with an explicit lesson using the first sample. Make explicit connections to the standard. Repeat with the other problems selected. After each of the problems, invite students to discuss the four PISA processes as they applied each to the problem. Conclude by inviting students to construct a real world problem aligned with this standard. Discuss the application of the four processes asking how students have improved each. End by making a poster (see www.glogster.com) that visually and publically defines the four processes: exploring and understanding, representing and formulating, planning and executing, and monitoring and reflecting (PISA, 2012). (Middle)

A Change of Culture. After reading a Harry Potter novel of choice, invite teams of three to put Harry and his chief adversary into a different country/culture/time. The teams will have to investigate the new culture and rewrite the story's ending for that country/culture/time. After presenting the new end of the story in appropriate costume, the team must explain the rationale for its choices including the alternatives they considered. (Middle-Cross-Curricular)

Problem First. Devise a sequence of questions to mediate student thinking after they finish reading a short story, novel, biography, narrative poem, or informational text. Focus the questions on the following, assigned before the start of the reading task:

- What was the problem faced by the main character? Provide text evidence.
- What thinking strategies did the character employ to resolve the problem? Provide text evidence.
- What alternatives might the character have considered? Explain your ideas. (Elementary-Middle)

Mediating Problem Definitions. Mediate student thinking about problem solving in a single Common Core State Standard ELA lesson or mini project. Use a website to brainstorm the topic for the essential problem statement. Provide students with a rubric that details the characteristics of a strong essential problem: (1) authentic or relevant to student interests; (2) open-ended but well-defined as possible; (3) drives the process; (4) matches with a standard. Next, brainstorm guiding questions that will help students resolve the problem statement about the topic. To close, discuss the value of making a problem as tightly defined as possible before discussing how they will use the problem defining skill in other situations. Probe with clarifying questions. (Middle-Secondary)

Problem of the Week. The 2003 PISA report provides a sample list of 13 exemplary mathematics problems (p. 56,¶92). To shift 9th- and 10th-grade students into the problem-solving mindset, select a problem per week for class work and discussion. Each month, select one of the processes (exploring, representing, etc.). In this case, build an explicit, multiday lesson, for the focus process. Use heterogeneous teams of three as the work unit. Be sure that students work through all 13 through the year, even though one problem is highlighted at a time. Have students keep a journal with notes about the strategies used for solving each problem. (Secondary)

On Your Own: Loosely Structured Challenges. Provide students with a loosely structured cross-curricular authentic problem (e.g., language arts, history, art) that fits with grade-appropriate instructional text/writing or speaking standards. Present a loosely structured project that will require teams of students to define the problem so that it is workable in time limits set, challenges students to employ at least three of the six thinking skills, and results in a product that shows the connection of the selected skills with the process of solving the problem. Allot time for each to present the solution and tools used to other members of the class. (Secondary)

A Problem Definition Rubric. Develop an age-appropriate rubric to present to the class at the start of the school year. Select one to four thinking skills appropriate for these students. At the end of each quarter, ask each student to reflect on his/her progress in using this skill to solve problems. Match the self-reflection with your use of the rubric to provide feedback to each student.

Connecting the Problem-Solving Dots. PISA 2012, the Common Core State Standards, and 21st-century thinking skills overlap in their goal of adding rigor to the curriculum by developing students' critical thinking and creative problem-solving skills. To help students keep a focus on this goal, make a poster that shows a problem-solving process that is nonsequentially arranged (see the list below). Either on a bulletin board (if you keep the same classroom) or in a journal (online or offline), invite students to start a concept map with the problem-solving process in the center (for online versions, go to www.bubbl.us). At times you select each quarter, facilitate the class's expansion of the concept map by finding online quotes that apply to the process or the contributory thinking skills and contributing ideas related to the meaning of the quotes. (All grades)

When displaying the 5-step problem-solving process, include these five elements listed below. Brainstorm with the class a way to design the visual so that it shows the items are not sequential steps, but an interactive flow among the elements. Pick the best design for the display of these five elements:

1. Define the problem.
2. Explore information and analyze information.
3. Design the most possible solution.
4. Test the proposed solution.
5. Conclude and Act.

As an option, create a class wiki. Again, on a regular basis, hold class discussions about problem solving and what students are learning about that process and the contributory skills highlighted.

IN SUMMARY

The PISA exams make concrete the challenges faced by American teachers. No longer are U.S. students solely in competition with their peers in North American schools. PISA demonstrates the increasing degree to which U.S. students are faced with competition not just on test scores, but for college seats and jobs in a global economy with peers from around the globe. The PISA exams spotlight the major rank of problem-solving competency in global students' repertoires. The Common Core Standards and the call for deeper learning highlight the importance of American students learning how to learn more rigorous content by applying and transferring the problem-solving skill set near and far across the curriculum and into the real world. To help students succeed with this challenge, American teachers will have to raise the level of their instructional game, and learn how to mediate problem solving for deeper learning.

Connecting the Dots

- List the three ideas from this chapter that are most meaningful to you.
- Explain why you selected each of these ideas.
- How might you transfer these ideas to your work with 21st-century learners?

> Don't find fault. Find a solution.
>
> —Henry Ford

APPENDIX A

Favorite Digital Sites to Promote Thinking and Problem-Solving Skills

Blogs: www.studentsoftheworld.info/sites/pages.php
Buck Institute of Education: www.bie.org
Class Tools: www.classtools.net
Common Core State Standards: www.corestandards.org/the-standards
Concept Maps and Brain Storming: www.bubbl.us
Cooperative Learning Institute: www.co-operation.org
Cyberbullying: www.Cyberbullying.Org.Nz
Don't Believe The Type: www.netsmartz.org
Edutopia: www.edutopia.org
Intel Teach: www.intel.com
International Renewal Institute, Inc.: www.iriinc.us
Journals: www.edailydiary.com
Language Arts: ReadWriteThink: www.readwritethink.org
Learning Games: www.learninggamesforkids.com
Mathematics: www.khanacademy.org
Mazes: www.clickmazes.com
Netsafe: www.Netsafe.Org.Nz/
New Tech Schools: www.newtechnetwork.org
Partnership for 21st Century Skills: www.P21.org
PISA: www.oecd.org
Portfolios: www.eportfolio.org
Posters: www.glogster.com
Robots: www.usFIRST.org
Science: http://beyondpenguins.ehe.osu.edu/

Science Simulations: http://phet.colorado.edu/en/simulations/index
Social Studies: Library of Congress: www.govdelivery.com
Survey/Polling: www.Pollyeverywhere.com or www.surveymonkey.com
Thinkfinity: www.thinkfinity.org
Thinkuknow: www.thinkuknow.co.uk

APPENDIX B

Feuerstein's List of Cognitive Functions

Focus Perception
Make and Test Hypotheses
Make Systematic Searches
Internalize
Label Like Groups
Test Alternative Strategies
Orient in Space
Choose Frame of Reference
Orient by Time
Plans with Goals
Conserve Constancies
Summarize a Concept
Measurement with Precision and Accuracy
Express a Concept
Integration of Information Sources
Express a Virtual Relationship
Identify and Define the Problem
Search for Alternatives
Select Relevant Information
Avoid Trial and Error Guesses
Make Spontaneous Comparisons
Control Impulsive Reactions
Connect Facts and Concepts
Form and Describe Categories
Employ Logical Evidence
Widen the Conceptual Field

Note: Adapted from Feuerstein, Feuerstein, and Falik, 2010.

Glossary

Advance Organizer: A high-effects strategy that is a crucial design element for inquiry projects and lessons. Includes tactics that call up prior knowledge before the start of a lesson or project.

Balanced Assessment: The evaluation of standards-based student performance that gives equal weight to the stated process skill (verb or verb form) and the content (direct object) in the standard.

Cognitive Engagement: The result of using instructional strategies that actively engage and develop the thinking functions and operations.

Cognitive Function: The Feuerstein term that includes 26 prerequisites of thinking used for thinking and problem solving across the curriculum.

Collaboration: Two or more persons working together with a common goal usually using a common approach or technology tool (e.g., blog, wiki).

Common Core State Standards: National performance benchmarks adopted by most states as a framework to guide balanced, rigorous instruction designed to advance academic and cognitive achievement and develop thinking skills and problem solving.

Communication: Interaction between two or more persons to share ideas, feelings, goals, and values about their mutual interests and work.

Constructive: The theory of learning which equates learning with the cognitive act of "making sense" of information via three mental phases: gathering information, making sense of information, and communicating new ideas.

Content: The facts, ideas, values, specific learning processes, and opinions that are the subject matter of any study in any discipline. Reading, writing, and arithmetic were the standard school content through the early 19th century. History, art, and other subjects blossomed after World War II and laid the stage for 21st-century content which includes financial, technological, and other literacies.

Creative Problem Solving: One of the basic four Cs of the 21st-century skill paradigm. CPS involves a series of cognitive sub-skills such as ideation and evaluation which are learned, refined, and applied to crucial issues in all disciplines. Attributes are fluency, flexibility, and divergence and with critical elements lead to solution of a problem.

Cross-Curricular Problem Solving: PISA 2012 term to describe problem solving that is not mathematical but addresses ill-defined problems across several disciplines.

Critical Thinking: Category of thinking operations and functions crucial in 21st-century learning experiences. Highlights convergent thinking processes such as analysis, compare, evaluation.

Deeper Learning: The result of instruction that intentionally develops critical thinking and creative problem-solving proficiencies in order to promote transfer of those skills and rigorous content across the curriculum and into real world scenarios.

Direct Instruction: A 19th-century model of teaching that received special attention in early school research as an effective model for helping students recall facts, procedures, and ideas for application with math operations and basic reading skills.

Engagement: The result of teachers using specific strategies and programs to keep students' attention on the material or content under study. The more advanced "cognitive engagement" is the result of specific strategies and programs designed to help students maintain focus on their complex cognitive skills.

Enriched Instruction: Specific approaches to instruction that are carried out with online and offline high-effects strategies identified by research to have the strongest effect on student achievement and complex cognitive skills.

Essential Question: The question that starts an inquiry or investigative project. Sometimes called the "driving" question or the "big" question since it always drives complex thinking about the topic or issue.

Explicit Instruction: This is instruction which purposefully helps students learn the definition, criteria, use, and assessment of a 21st-century skill prior to its application in a lesson or project. Leads to facilitated application and mediation of thinking/problem-solving skills. Teacher may use direct instruction model or inquiry model to frame the lesson or project.

Focus: The essential cognitive function that allows learners or workers to concentrate intensely on one task at a time.

Formative Assessment: Determination of development in a lesson or project to identify progress and to provide constructive feedback.

Four Cs: Four 21st-century skill categories identified by P21: critical thinking, creative problem solving, communication, and collaboration.

Gaming: The development and/or use of game design to teach content and develop problem-solving skills in the curriculum.

Gathering Information: The first phase of thinking in the constructivist learning framework. Includes skills and attitudes that enable students to collect and evaluate needed data to answer an essential question or define a problem. Relies on multiple sources of data including prior knowledge, written text, visuals, enactments, lectures, etc.

High Effect: Those instructional strategies that effects studies determine have the greatest chance to raise student achievement.

Inquiry: The process of investigating a fact, topic, process, procedure, concept, or value so as to understand the investigation's focus more deeply.

Innovative Thinking: The cognitive process that enables the invention of different products that are substantively different from existing models.

Intentional: Describes the purposeful teaching or use of a specific instructional strategy, tool, or tactic to deepen content knowledge or complex skill acquisition.

Investigation: See Inquiry.

Mediated Learning Experience: A term used by Feuerstein that describes how teachers have focused student learning on thinking and problem-solving skills.

Phase: A major segment of the constructivist learning process that includes a variety of cognitive strategies, tools, and tactics needed to produce desired end results in measurable products, understandings, or skill developments. There are three phases: gathering information, making sense, and communicating new ideas.

PISA: The Program for International Student Assessment that tests 15-year-olds from 30-member countries. In 2012 the tests of mathematics problem solving, reading literacy, and science literacy were joined by exams of financial literacy and cross-curricular problem solving. PISA tests are computer based.

Practical Strategy: A learning activity that is planted in a model of teaching intentionally to advance student learning. *Practical* implies that a large number of teachers see that the activity is highly transferable with adjustments to teach content or skills in any discipline.

Problem-Based Learning: A project-based learning model of instruction that starts with a loosely defined problem and ends with a solution or result.

Problem Definition: This is a cognitive function that is the first process in problem solving.

Problem Solving: The set of interactive critical and creative thinking strategies aligned to provide a solution to a problem that may range from being loosely to tightly structured. Loosely structured problems are those that require investigation and refinement into a specific problem statement because the situation is considered "messy" (e.g., water pollution). A tightly structured problem provides the specific definition of the problem (e.g., mathematics).

Product-Based Learning: A project-based learning model of instruction that begins with an idea for a new or innovative product that fulfills a specific, defined need. This mode is built around the making and testing of an innovative product that meets a market need

Project-Based Learning: Is the category that includes the problem-based, product-based, and inquiry-based learning models of instruction. The project-based model answers an important or essential question through the investigation of data that ends with an answer.

Systemic Search: The essential cognitive function used to exam data in an orderly way.

21st-Century School: This is a school that intentionally creates a curriculum that investigates 21st-century issues, explicitly teaches 21st-century skills, and employs inquiry to examine standards-based content 100% of the time for all students.

Understanding: The result of learning rigorous and relevant content through development of 21st-century skills applied to authentic content. Understanding is not a plateau. Understanding exists on a spectrum that proceeds from slim, shallow, and slight to deep, dependent upon the length and seriousness of the investigation.

Web 2.0: These are free Internet tools that enable teachers to better manage and develop students' learning in a 21st-century classroom. Web 2.0 tools provide a range of readiness for easy to advanced adoption by students.

References

American College Testing Service. (2012). The condition of college and career readiness. Retrieved from http://www.act.org/readiness

American Management Association (2010). Critical skills survey. Retrieved from http:www.P.21.org/storage.

Bellanca, J. (2010). *Enriched learning projects.* Bloomington, IN: Solution Tree Press.

Bellanca, J., Fogarty, R., & Pete, B. (2012). *How to teach thinking within the Common Core Standards.* Bloomington, IN: Solution Tree Press.

Bellanca, J., Paul, A., & Paul, M. (2012). *On becoming a self-directed learner.* Northbrook, IL: International Renewal Press.

Ben Hur, M. (2006). *Concept rich mathematics.* Alexandria, VA: Association for Supervision and Curriculum Development.

Billstein, R., Libeskind, S., & Lott, J.W. (2010). A problem-solving approach to mathematics for elementary school teachers (10th Ed.). Old Tappan, NJ: Pearson Higher Education Publications.

Bransford, J. D., Brown, A. O., & Cockling, R. R. (Eds.). (1999). *How people learn: Brain, mind, experience, and school.* Washington, DC: National Academy Press.

Buccino, G., Binkofski, F., & Riggio, L. (2004). The mirror neuron systems and action recognition. *Brain and Language, 89*(2), 370–376.

Clark, R., Shuman, L. J., Besterfield-Sacre, M. (2009). Indepth use of modeling in engineering coursework to enhance problem solving. In R., Lesh, P. L. Galbraith, C. R. Haines, & G. Kaiser (Eds.), *Modeling students mathematical competencies.* New York: Springer Science.

Coch, D. & Ansari, D. (2006). Bridges over troubled waters: Education and cognitive neuroscience. *Trends in Cognitive Sciences, 10*(4). Retrieved from http://numericalcognition.org/wp-content/uploads/2010/08/Ansari-Coch_TICS20061.pdf

Common Core State Standards (n.d.) Retrieved from http://www.corestandards.org

Conley, D. T. (2007). *Toward a more comprehensive conception of college readiness.* Eugene, OR: Educational Policy Improvement Center.

Coyle, J. (2013). YouTube has already defeated TV, Google's Eric Schmidt says. *Denver Post.* Retrieved from http://www.denverpost.com/technology/ci_23164841/youtube-has-already-defeated-tv-googles-eric-schmidt

Daniels, H., Zemmelman, S., and Hyde, A. (2005). *Best practices: Today's standards for teaching.* Portsmouth, NH: Heinemann.

Darling-Hammond, L. D. (2011). *Powerful learning: What we know about teaching and learning.* San Francisco: John Wiley and Sons.

Davidson, J., and Sternberg, R. (Eds.). (2003). *The psychology of problem solving.* New York: Cambridge University Press.

De Bono, E. (1999). *Six thinking hats.* Boston: Little Brown and Company.

Denver Green School. (2012) "Plants and worms," Mastery project outline, Denver Green School. Retrieved from www.ilc21.org/resources/free templates

Dryden, K. (2003). *The game.* Toronto: Trigraphic Printing, Ltd. (Original work published 1983)

Efkilides, A., & Misaldi, P. (Eds.). (2010), *Trends and prospects in metacognitve research.* New York: Springer.

Fogarty, R., and Pete, B. (2005). *How to differentiate learning.* Thousand Oaks: Corwin Press.

Feuerstein, R., Feuerstein, R., & Falik, L. (2010). *Beyond smarter.* New York: Teachers College Press.

Feuerstein, R., Rand, Y., Hoffman, M., & Miller, R. (1980). *Instrumental enrichment.* Baltimore, MD: University Park Press.

Frontline. (2012) Dropout nation. Retrieved from http://dropoutnation.net/

Guilford, J. P. (1971). *The analysis of intelligence.* San Francisco: McGraw-Hill.

Harvard Graduate School of Education. (2011). Pathways to prosperity. Retrieved from http://www.gse.harvard.edu

Hewlett Foundation. (2012). Definition of deeper learning. Retrieved from http://www.hewlett.org/deeperlearning

Holt, C. (1999, January). Teaching economics with classroom experiments. *Southern Economic Journal, 65*(3), 603–610.

Immordino-Yang, M. H., Chiao, J. Y., & Fiske, A. P. (2010). Neural re-use in the social and emotional brain. *Brain and Behavioral Sciences, 33*(4), 275–276.

Johnson, D.W., & Johnson, R. (2004).Implemening the teaching students to be peacemakers program. *Theory Into Practice, 43*(1).

Kao, J. (2007). *Innovation nation.* New York: Free Press.

Kermin, S. (1979, June). Teacher expectations and student achievement. *Phi Delta Kappan, 60*(10), 716–718.

Lemke, C. (2011). *What every educator should know about technology.* Retrieved from http://eschoolnews.com

Lesh, R., and Zawojewski, J. S. (2007). Problem solving and modeling. In F. Lester (Ed.), *The handbook of research on mathematics teaching and learning* (2nd ed.) (pp. 763–804). Reston, VA: National Council of Teachers of Mathematics and Charlotte, NC: Information Age Publishing (joint publication).

Linan-Thompson, S. (2010). IES practice guide: Improving reading comprehension in kindergarten through 3rd grade. Reading Keynote. Retrieved from http:////ctl.uoregon.edu/pd/cf11/strands/reading/keynote_reading_comprehension

Marden, O.S. (2010). Bell telephone talk. In How They Succeeded. Whitefish, MT: Kessinger. (Original published 1901.)

Marzano Research Lab (2012). Researched strategies. Retrieved from http// www.marzanoresearchlab.com

Mayer, R. E., & Wittrock, M. C. (2006). Problem solving. In P. A. Alexander and P. Winne (Eds.), *Handbook of educational psychology* (2nd ed.). Mahwah, NJ: Lawrence Erlbaum Associates.

McGraw Hill Research Foundation. (2011). Growing demand for a skillful and educated global workforce. Retrieved from http://www.McGrawhhillresearch foundation.org

McTighe, J., & Wiggins, G. (2005). *Understanding by design* (2nd ed.). Alexandria, VA: Association for Supervision and Curriculum Development.

Meier, D. (2011). The teacher–student relationship: Our most important data source. Retrieved from http://www.uknow.gse.harvard.edu/leadership/LP101-407.htm

Mergendoller, J. (2012). "Does project-based-learning teach critical thinking?" Retrieved from www.p21.org/blog.

Norberg, P. (Ed.). (2004). *The complete works of Ralph Waldo Emerson.* New York: Barnes and Noble Classics.

P21. (2012). Mile Guide, Partnership for 21st Century Skills. Retrieved from http://www.p21.org/storage/documents/MILE_Guide_091101.pdf

Pellegrino, J. & Hilton, M. (2012) *Education for life and work: Developing transferable knowledge and skills in the 21st Century.* Washington, DC: National Academies Press.

Polya, G. (2012). *How to solve it: A new aspect of mathematical method.* Princeton, NJ: Princeton Press. (Original work published 1945)

Programme for International Student Assessment (PISA). (2003). First results from PISA 2003. Retrieved from http://www.oecd.org/dataoecd/1/63/34002454.pdf

Programme for International Student Assessment (PISA). (2009). Key findings. Key findings. Retrieved fromhttp://www.oecd.org/pisa/pisaproducts/pisa2009keyfindings.htm

Programme for International Student Assessment (PISA). (2011). Learning beyond fifteen: 10 years after PISA. Retrieved from http://pisa.oecd.org

Programme for International Student Assessment (PISA). (2012). Framework for problem solving 2012. Retrieved from http://www.oecd.org

Ravitz, J. (2009). Does PBL work? A meta-analysis. Buck Institute of Education. Retrieved from http://www.bie.org/research/study/does_pbl_work

Richter, J. P. Ed. (1970). *The notebooks of Leonardo da Vinci, Volume 1*. Mineola, NY: Dover. (Original work published 1888)

Rizzolatti, G., & Arbib, M. A. (1998). Language within our grasp. *Trends in Neurosciences, 21*(5), 188–194.

Schacter, J. (1999). *The impact of education technology on student achievement: What the most current research has to say.* Santa Monica, CA: Milkin Family Fund.

Schneider, M., & Lin, Y. (2011). High cost of low graduation rates. *American Institute of Research.* Retrieved from http://www.air.org.

Sternberg, R. (1998). *Handbook of creativity.* New York: Cambridge University Press.

Sternberg, R. (1999). *Thinking styles.* New York: Cambridge University Press.

Sternberg, R., & Grigorenko, E. (2007). *Teaching for successful intelligence* (2nd ed.). Thousand Oaks, CA: Corwin Press.

Stewart, S. (2006). Are they really ready to work? Final report. Retrieved from http://www.p21.org/storage/documents/FINAL_REPORT_PDF09-29-06.pdf

Toyota Business Process. (2010) The eight steps for successful problem solving. Retrieved from http://www.accountability.wa.gov/leadership/lean/documents/

Wagner, A. (2010). *The global achievement gap: Why even our best schools don't teach the skills our children need.* New York: Basic Books.

Willis, J. (2010). Current impact of neuroscience on teaching and learning. In D. Sousa (Ed.), *Minds, brains, and education.* Bloomington, IN: Solution Tree Press.

Vogt S., Ritzl, A., Fink, G.R., Zilles K., Freund, H. J., & Rizzolatti, G. (2004). Neural circuits underlying imitation learning of hand actions: An event related MRI study. *Neuron, 42*, 323–334.

Vygotsky, L. S. (1978). *Mind in society: The development of higher psychological processes* (M. Cole, V. John-Steiner, S. Scribner, & E. Souberman, Eds.) Cambridge, MA: Harvard University Press.

Zimmer, R., Gill, G., Booker, K., Lavertu, S., Sass, T., & Witte, J. (2009). *Charter schools in eight states: Effects on achievement, attainment, integration, and competition.* Santa Monica, CA: RAND Corporation.

Zipkes, S. (2012). *New thinking for new schools for the 21st century: What will it take?* P21 Blog Post. Washington, DC. Retrieved from http://www.p21.org/tools-and-resources/p21blog

Index

About the Author

James A. Bellanca is a practical innovator who thinks ahead of the curve and provides teachers and administrators with the knowledge to make abstract ideas concrete and ready to go on the next school day. Among his colleagues, he is recognized for his ability to foresee coming trends in education and connect best current classroom practices with what's needed by teachers who are committed to innovative excellence.

With his extensive experience as a classroom English and language arts teacher, alternative school director, professional developer, intermediate service center director, business owner, and not-for-profit executive, Jim has consistently focused on developing students' abilities for learning how to learn, think, and problem solve not only for their benefits but as powerful learning tools that can be utilized for all. A leading voice in twenty-first–century skills, Jim is lead blogger for the Partnership for 21st Century Schools (P21) blog, "Connecting the 21st Century Dots: From Policy to Practice." He is executive director of the Illinois Consortium for 21st Century Schools and is lead trainer for Mind Quest: Project Based Learning in the 21st Century Classroom. In addition, Jim is lead trainer of instructors for the New York State United Teachers Education Learning Trust program, "The 21st Century Classroom." In the past year, he has designed three online graduate education courses and the innovative online workshop, "Projects from a Box" and most recently coauthored a leaders' guide for integrating 21st-century skills with the Common Core.